The

and

Martial

Arts

by Carl Brown

© 1998 Ohara Publications, Inc.
All rights reserved
Printed in the United States of America
Library of Congress Catalog Number: 97-069903
ISBN: 0-89750-134-9

Second printing 1999

WARNING

OHARA [] PUBLICATIONS, INCORPORATED

SANTA CLARITA, CALIFORNIA

DEDICATION

This book is dedicated to the Honorable John W. Wade, to my judo *sensei* Richard "Dick" Falls, to my *imua kuon-tao* kung fu instructor Sgt. Joseph O'Hara and to *o-sensei* (major teacher) of judo Phil Porter.

The late Dean John Wade—Dean Emeritus and Distinguished Professor of Law Emeritus, Vanderbilt University School of Law and reporter of The Restatement of Torts, 2d.—passed away in 1996, and it is fitting that this book is dedicated to the lasting memory of, in my opinion, one of the most profound legal scholars of the 20th century.

Dean John Wade is pictured here with author Carl Brown upon Brown's graduation from Vanderbilt University School of Law in 1976. Brown's dissertation was about the martial arts and the law.

Were it not for his guidance and encouragement, this book would not be on the shelves.

Dean Wade, known affectionately to us Vanderbilt Law students as "The Cobra," taught tort law in all its many forms to thousands of aspiring lawyers. Despite the demands placed on his time by legal academicians, his considerable writings, his teachings and his administrative load, Dean Wade always found time to advise his student charges.

I will always remember sheepishly entering his office for the first time to ask if (strict) product liability law had been adopted by

Tennessee. He leaned back in his chair, closed his eyes, and gave me, from memory, not only the name of the case but the numerical citation where it could be found!

His brilliance was eclipsed by his kindness and common sense approach to law and policy questions. He will be missed.

Sensei Richard "Dick" Falls, the man who began teaching me judo in 1963, was a leading light of Louisville judo, one of the first judo instructors in Kentucky. Back then, judo was almost synonymous with martial arts in this country, so he was a pioneer for all martial artists. He founded the Louisville Judo Club where, even today, at the same location, other old-timers and I

Richard "Dick" Falls the author's Judo sensei, in a jujitsu fighting stance.

study under the able instruction of sensei Mike Royse, sixth *dan*, at the Toshi Judo and Jujitsu Dojo. Sensei Falls taught me the budo way and placed my twelve-year-old feet firmly on "the path up the mountain."

The dedication must be expanded further to include my imua kuon-tao kung fu instructor, Sgt. Joseph O'Hara, who left a booming martial arts club in the 1960s to go to Vietnam, where he could, as a soldier, practice his martial art to its fullest extent. Bushido Judo was born of this judo and kung fu marriage, and I owe *sifu* O'Hara honor and respect for his hard-style contribution.

In conclusion, I dedicate this book as well to o-sensei Phil Porter, ninth dan judo black belt and former president of both the United States Judo Association and the National Judo Institute. I have not had the joy of working out with o-sensei since the '70s, but now that he is in his 70s, I would have less of a chance to beat him! He has brought judo from obscurity and open warfare among

The man breaking is Joseph O'Hara

national associations to producing Olympic medalists. Judo training is now available not only in Colorado Springs at the National Judo Institute headquarters, but also throughout America at summer camps. The USJA has recently expanded its membership to include other martial arts.

To Dean Wade, sensei Falls, sifu O'Hara and o-sensei Porter: Thank you for each in your own way making this book a reality.

ACKNOWLEDGMENTS

First things first: my thanks go to many people for making this book possible:

1. To the late Mike Lee, my first assigned editor, who worked with me during the early stages of this book and who died a violent death at the hands of California thugs. Mike, I miss you;

2. To Deborah Overman, who filled the large shoes of Mike Lee and helped give birth to this book;

3. To Kentucky lawyers Murray Porath and Kathy Munroe for solid assistance with the research;

4. To all those attorneys out there with the moxie to take appeals of these dozens—almost 200—cases dealing with martial artists and their legal woes; in 1975, when I finished my research for my juris doctorate thesis at the Vanderbilt University School of Law, there were only four cases directly dealing with martial artists. The cases in this book represent literally thousands of hours of legal research done by the lawyers of America. I am merely the chronicler;

5. To Vanderbilt Law School's Dean Emeritus and Distinguished Professor of Law Emeritus John W. Wade and Professor Karl Warden, for whom I did the tandem papers that gave rise to the first book, which was published in 1983;

6. To Tom Jackson for his help at the University of Louisville Library, finding legal authority and lugging books to the copy machine like some legal mule;

7. To my assistant, Richard Loeb, longtime student and friend. He's the *uke* taking the punishment in most of the photos contained in this book. My thanks for his loyalty, professionalism and skill;

At threshhold, it must be stressed that there is no substitute for advice of local counsel. Statutes change, and so do court rulings. My particular "spin" on the law may or may not ring true with a judge or prosecutor. Seek legal advice in your home state, if the need arises. Hopefully, this book will be of aid to your lawyer—but it begins and not ends the inquiry.

ABOUT THE AUTHOR

Carl Brown began his martial arts training in 1956 at the age of five in the backyard of a friend, whose older brother taught from a book he purchased at a drug store. In 1963, at age twelve, Brown began his formal *kodokan* judo training with teacher Richard Falls at the YMCA in downtown Louisville. He also studied *imua kuon-tao* kung fu (way of the forward fist).

He competed in various tournaments during his teenage years. At the YMCA Southern Area Games, a competition between YMCA martial arts clubs from the South, he won second place in the heavy-weight division in 1967 and won first place in the heavyweight division in 1968 and 1969, to become "heavyweight champion of the South." Brown received his black belt from the United States Judo Federation in 1973 and has been teaching judo since then. Brown is also affiliated with the United States Judo Association and United States Judo, Inc. He has taught martial arts in five states, and in 1995

instructed judo and kung fu at the University of Louisville Bushido Judo Club. In 1998, at age 47, he still competes on the tournament circuit in the judo masters division.

In 1976, Brown received his Juris Doctorate from the Vanderbilt University School of Law, graduating near the top of his class. While in law school, he wrote legislation creating the Tennessee Energy Office and drafted lobbying reform legislation for Kentucky.

Brown ceased actively practicing law in April 1986 and has since devoted his efforts to writing. He has written extensively for several national martial arts magazines, including *Black Belt, Karate/Kung Fu Illustrated* and *Martial Arts Training,* as well as other non-martial arts magazines. He intends to resume a part-time law practice in 1998.

As set forth in the 1985 *Black Belt Magazine Yearbook,* Brown developed a form of judo known as Bushido Judo, a blend of imua kuon-tao kung fu techniques with judo throws, arm locks, chokes and pins. Further, Brown's study of the world classic *Go Rin No Sho* (*A Book of Five Rings*) by Miyamoto Musashi led him to interesting application in the martial arts field. Musashi's book deals with strategy and is studied at the Harvard Business School as a key text on Japanese business techniques.

Brown posited that while Musashi's text dealt with swordsmanship, the principles could be extended to the type of response to attack. In self-defense and the defense of others, one must offer a proportionate response, that is, no more than necessary. Brown teaches the Water, Earth, Air, Fire and The Void responses to attack. This is taught by Brown as the "W.E.A.F.V. warrior way" and comports the conduct of martial artists to the "no excessive force" requirements of the law, as set forth in this text.

In short, WATER is defense by judo, *jujitsu* and *aikido.* EARTH is defense by absorbing the punishment. AIR is not being there when the blow lands. FIRE is defense by karate, *wushu* and *taekwondo.* THE VOID is defense by *ninjutsu.*

In addition to practicing law, Brown served as Jefferson County Commissioner from 1979 to 1983 and was one of only four people who set policy in the metropolitan Louisville area. Brown was one of the youngest persons to ever have the privilege to serve his community in such a vital position. While Jefferson

VANDERBILT UNIVERSITY
NASHVILLE, TENNESSEE 37240

School of Law

Carl Brown prepared a dissertation for me on the Material Arts and the Law of Torts some time back. It was comprehensive and well done. Now he has broadened its coverage but he still shows a true scholar's thorough-ness and an ability to communicate well with the layman.

I predict success for the book.

John W. Wade
John W. Wade
Dean Emeritus and Distinguished
Professor of Law Emeritus,
Vanderbilt University
School of Law

County Commissioner, Brown served on the Board of Directors of both the Boys Club Council and State YMCA of Kentucky, on the Board of Overseers of the University of Louisville and on NASA's Land Satellite Task Force. Brown was also named "Outstanding Young Kentuckian" and "Outstanding Young American," and served as the youngest state delegation head to the once-a-decade White House Conference on Youth.

He has taught both undergraduate judo and graduate political science courses at the University of Louisville as well as high school debate.

Known as "The Plain Brown Rapper," Brown editorializes twice weekly on Louisville radio station WQMF, voted in 1995 the most popular station in the Louisville area.

He also has his own Louisville cable television show, "The Plain Brown Rapper: The Revolution is Now Televised". His guests range from Navy SEALS to Governors and congressmen, cross-dressers to martial arts masters and faith healers.

Brown's radio editorial is repeated on the TKR-8 cable show and in Louisville's critically acclaimed Louisville Eccentric Observer, an alternative tabloid that is Kentucky's largest weekly newspaper. He is known for his fearless rant against those who in his opinion, misstep.

INTRODUCTION

In the ongoing debate that takes place in martial arts circles, one argues about the purpose of one's training. Admittedly, most people join self-defense schools to learn to defend themselves without using weapons. Although thousands of martial artists are interested in character-building, physical fitness and mental well-being, most Americans enter the local *dojo* (martial arts training hall) originally as a way to feel more confident about their ability to protect themselves.

This leads to some questions: Do you have an automatic right to defend yourself in any way that you feel is necessary? Are you immune to assault and battery charges or civil lawsuits brought against you by someone you injured while defending yourself? If threatened with harm, are you justified in taking any action you deem necessary to protect yourself, your sweetheart or your automobile?

All who presently train in the martial arts should be aware of some specific court rulings that might bear on their actions. You don't have as many simple, clear-cut rights as you think. Brandishing your martial arts skills may lead to an arrest, or a costly and complicated lawsuit.

This is why I wrote this book. There are legal ramifications in defending yourself, be it in your home, a neighborhood bar, a parking lot or elsewhere. Different legal constraints may apply to your actions. And remember, the courts always assume you are aware of the legal limits of your actions. The old legal maxim, "Ignorance of the law is no defense," applies here as well.

American law varies from state to state, and some laws have changed only slightly in a century. Others have changed from year to year, as new circumstances arise. While no book can claim to cover all the issues relating to physical action while defending yourself, this book can help you sort out the major legal questions.

In this book, I examine the record of American law concerning assault and battery, and explain what legally defines excessive force, what reasonable presumptions apply to self-defense, and what constitutes an "anticipatory attack" (attacking when you believe you will be attacked if you don't act). I also detail special areas for the "trained fighter" and explain why he may be held accountable because a standard (which I will also explain) governing his actions is applied. A court may consider a black belt to be a self-defense "expert," so the rules regarding how well he judged the force of his reaction are stiffer.

Some courts expect an individual to retreat before taking any violent physical action. If you're capable of escaping from an attacker, you should do so before breaching the peace. There's one important exception, and that's when you've been confronted by an intruder in your home. In this case, you have the right not to retreat.

I provide many examples of court cases which illuminate legal trends, and tell you how you can expect to be treated if you overstep your legal boundaries. It's important that you know what could happen if you do defend yourself violently.

While I give some hypothetical examples, and offer advice based upon legal precedents and my own professional experience, this book cannot be considered a cure-all. It will not protect you from a lawsuit or criminal charges, and it does not intend to be a substitute for good legal counsel. However, it can guide you through the complicated maze of law as it relates to self-defense.

If you ever have to defend yourself with force, and doing so lands you in a court battle, you should get an attorney. There's no substitute for a competent lawyer who is skilled in the law and experienced in the courtroom. That's an entirely different skill than what's used on the street.

Technique photos: Doug Churchill
All other photos, courtesy of Carl Brown

Proofreaders: Deborah Overman
                Sara Fogan
Graphic Design: Blumhoff Design

CONTENTS

CHAPTER ONE

The Martial Arts

Interest in the martial arts is exploding in the United States. At the outset, it is interesting to note that when we speak of "martial," we refer to something "of, relating to, or suited for war." In contrast, the Japanese word for martial is comprised of two components: "stop" and "spear," depicting "martial" in a purely defensive sense.

This chapter explores the four arts believed to be most prevalent in America: karate, *jujitsu,* judo and *aikido.* Naturally, however, the "American arts" of boxing and wrestling, while not singled out for discussion, also produce trained fighters.

Karate is both a fighting art and a sport. Its name is comprised of the Japanese words *kara* (empty) and *te* (hands)—thus, karate means to fight weaponless—with "empty hands." The origins of karate have been obscured. Some contend its development can be traced to Okinawa, although the basic concept of karate was borrowed from Chinese boxing. Others focus on its relatively late Japanese influence where, disarmed by an Emperor's decree, peasants trained secretly to overcome the armor of the samurai, the warriors and bodyguards of the *daimyo.*

In the most widely held and authoritative view, karate's origins are traced to the ingenuity of Indian and Chinese monks who had the dilemma of making trade journeys through dangerous, bandit-laden mountains while restricted by their religion from lifting weapons against other human beings. These monks conditioned their bodies into potent weapons for self-defense. By pounding their hands and feet on rocks, they transformed their natural appendages into deadly, club-like weapons. Legend has it that the monks, after disarming and battering their surprised assailants, would bandage and comfort the bandits before resuming their journey. A Buddhist monk named Bodhidharma is most often credited as the founder of this weaponless fighting art, which is the forerunner of karate.

Karateka (karate practitioners) attack and defend both in contest and on the street, not only with punches and open-hand blows, but also with their knees, elbows and feet, and even their head. Punches and kicks are the most frequently used techniques. The punches are straight, directed along the body's centerline, and tend

A karate corkscrew punch.

to be thrown with an exaggerated hip movement to get full body weight behind the blow. Kicks are slower but more powerful and deceptive. The angle of approach is difficult to predict. For example, a front kick starts with the knee raised to the chest, but from there one can assault the groin with a front snap kick, or strike the skull with a roundhouse kick. Many karateka, like their Buddhist monk predecessors, toughen their hands and feet. Typically, a *makiwara* (a large flat board with extra wood and padding attached) is used for this purpose. Methodical kicking and punching of the makiwara toughen the feet and edges of the hands. Upon delivery of a technique, karateka utter yells known as *kiai.* This serves the dual purpose of startling the opponent and stimulating the karateka's own adrenaline flow.

There are numerous styles of martial arts. By country, the Japanese, Chinese and Korean styles command the greatest following among hundreds of thousands of practitioners. To name a few, *shotokan, goju-ryu, shito-ryu, kenpo, tae kwon do* and kung fu are prominent Oriental "boxing" styles practiced by Americans. The latter two deserve special mention. Although tae kwon do's origins are ultimately traceable to China, as are the other styles, many Koreans take exception to this style being lumped together with other forms of karate, apparently more for reasons of nationalism than logic. In a similar vein, many kung fu artists resist being labeled "karateka," since kung fu is a general term encompassing many styles of Chinese boxing. Karate and kung fu do share some fundamental hand-and-foot techniques, but kung fu lays greater stress than karate on finger blows (clawing and stabbing) to the eyes and throat. Whether fact or fiction, some kung fu practitioners of old claim the legendary ability to deliver "death touches." These distinctions notwithstanding, for the purposes of this book, "karate" will include any Oriental martial art which teaches hand blows and kicks.

These hand blows and kicks are potent forces. Peasants of feudal Okinawa could subdue armed opponents with their bare hands and feet. It is widely believed that a karate expert's hands can be as lethal as a hammer. Although vast numbers of Americans have witnessed

A *jujitsu* arm lock.

karateka break amazing amounts of wood, brick, stone and ice, few have witnessed the awesome power displayed dramatically by men such as Mas Oyama, a major figure in karate's development. Oyama killed a bull with his bare hands, proving karate can be dangerous for bricks, boards, *and* living things.

Unlike karate and judo, *jujutsu,* more commonly known as jujitsu, only recently developed a sport dimension. It is largely raw self-defense. However, the Japanese term means "art of softness." This

The judo throw *haraigoshi.*

seeming inconsistency is resolved in that the jujitsu artist defeats his or her opponent by "appearing to yield." Like karate, there is no small dispute about the origin of jujitsu among historians.

Some claim jujitsu paralleled the development of karate and was originated by Buddhist monks for protection against marauders. More probable, however, is that jujitsu was developed indigenous to Japan and dates back as far as 230 B.C. No less a scholar than Dr. Jigoro Kano, the founder of judo (which is the clear and direct descendant of jujitsu), states conclusively that jujitsu differed so radically from karate that it could not have come from China; rather, it developed in Japan when peasants were forbidden to wear swords. Eventually, the samarai were compelled to learn jujitsu. It became part of their code of honor to attempt to defeat their opponents with jujitsu before drawing their sword.

As indicated, jujitsu is largely for self-defense. Jujitsu teaches how to throw, choke, lock joints and hold—these latter four elements forming the basis for judo.

Judo, now part of the Olympic games, is practiced more as a sport than for self-defense, although its utility for self-defense is unquestioned. Judo (the gentle way) is "the art of appearing to give way." Knowledgeable historians unanimously concur that judo was derived from jujitsu and systemized in 1882 by Jigoro Kano, an eminent Japanese physical educator and lecturer. Kano refined the harsh jujitsu techniques, purging them of their inherently deadly aspects, and added new techniques of his own. The test of fire came for Kano's new system in 1886. Declining jujitsu schools resented the growing popularity of judo. Fifteen of Kano's students and 15 of the best jujitsu practitioners from the outstanding Totsuka School competed in a national tournament under the auspices of the Metropolitian Police Department. Kano's *judoka* (judo practitioners) reigned supreme, winning 13 of the matches and drawing two.

Kano put forth two great judo principles: (1) maximum efficiency with minimum effort, and (2) mutual benefit and welfare. These principles were the two pillars of the "code of humanitarian ethics" that he contributed to the martial arts. This code, and the gentleness of its propagator, is best illustrated by his final match. During a voyage to Europe, Kano, a short, slight man, met a huge Russian in a wrestling match. To the dismay of the spectators, who expected the Russian to easily overpower the small Japanese, Kano threw his opponent effortlessly. To make this all the more remarkable, he placed his hand under the Russian's head to keep him from hurting it on the floor when he fell. Despite the international popularity of the man and his art, Kano was poisoned as his ship sailed between America and Japan. The circumstances of his death are still mysterious. Today, Kano's picture hangs in most judo *dojo,* and all students bow to his image before and after each class as a show of respect.

Although it's difficult to determine precisely the number of judoka in America, judo commands an impressive following. As both an Olympic and an AAU (American Athletic Union) sport, its ranks have increased impressively. Judo appeals to the young and old and to persons in all walks of life. Kyuzo Mifune, a great moving influence in judo, practiced actively until his death at age 81. And Theodore Roosevelt worked out regularly at the White House under a protege of Kano, and gained exceptional skill.

Judo's characterization as "gentle" is deceptive. It is very rough and effective. However, the muscular strength so vital to boxing and wrestling is less important in judo. In fact, the weight and strength of *your opponent* provides all that is needed for his or her defeat since you use your opponent's weight against him. This opening gambit of non-resistance contains a built-in element of surprise, since no attacker expects an opponent to fight back by yielding. Judo instructors teach throws, pins, chokes and armlocks. Judo is unique in that judoka may practice with wild abandon since they are taught how to fall without injury and how to submit when a choke, hold or armlock becomes dangerous. In contest judo, a premium is placed on the coordination between body movement and mental strategy, making judo like a game of chess. No available synopsis of judo is better than that given by Jigoro Kano himself in a speech before a University of Southern California audience, on the occasion of the Tenth Olympiad, 1932:

Let me now explain what this gentleness or giving way really means. Suppose we assume that we may estimate the strength of man in units of one. Let us say that the strength of man standing in front of me is represented by ten units, whereas my strength, less than his, is represented by seven units. Then if he pushes me with all his force I shall certainly be pushed back or thrown down, even if I use all my strength against him. This would happen because I used all my strength against him, opposing strength with strength. But if, instead of opposing him, I were to give way to strength by withdrawing my body just as much as he had pushed remembering to keep my balance, then he would naturally lean forward and thus lose his balance. In this new position, he may have become weak (not in actual physical strength but because of his awkward position) as to have his strength represented for the moment by, say, only three units, instead of his normal ten units. But meanwhile, I, by keeping my balance, retain my full strength, as originally represented by seven units. Here then, I am momentarily in an advantageous position and I can defeat my opponent using only half of my strength, that is half of my seven units, or three and one-half of my strength against his three. This leaves one-half (units) of my strength available for any purpose. In case I had greater strength than my opponent I could of course push him back. But even in this case, that is, if I had wished to push him back and had the power to do so, it would be better first for me to have given way, because in doing so I should have greatly economized my energy.

Aikido is the most mystical martial art. Founded in 1925 by Japan's Morihei Uyeshiba, it is the most modern of Japan's fighting arts. Aikido

An *aikido* wrist lock.

means "accumulated force," the unity of thought and action. This fluid, circular, potent martial art is based on the thought that all body movements agree with the laws of nature. Aikido teaches throws, wristlocks, armlocks and escapes, applied in circular rather than linear movements.

The popularity and on-screen exploits of actor and aikido stylist Steven Seagal has increased the recognition of this art.

Clearly, boxing, wrestling, *sumo,* etc., qualify as much as fighting arts as the Japanese arts previously discussed. However, for the purpose of discussion, this book will concentrate on the Oriental arts of self-defense (and offense). Nevertheless, it is important to stress that *trained fighters* are the focus of this book, regardless of the specific art or arts in which one becomes proficient.

CHAPTER TWO

Assault
and
Battery

Of all the topics in this book, this is the most difficult to discuss. A trained fighter should be the last one to ever use his or her skills in an aggressive, unprovoked manner. Happily, such instances are rare in the martial arts world. This is no doubt due to the discipline instilled in martial artists by the ethics of the Oriental arts (and the calm that comes from attaining black belt or "expert" status). But whether or not you are the actual cause of a physical incident, you may still be accused of assault and battery.

Assault and battery is two-faceted: the civil offense and the criminal offense. Further, although it is usually mentioned in the same breath, assault and battery are separate offenses. Simply put, *assault* is

An "assault" is acting in such a way as to put another person in imminent danger of physical harm. Technically, author Carl Brown has "assaulted" his assistant by dropping into a fighting stance.

acting in such a way as to put another in *imminent apprehension* of physical harm. *Battery* is carrying through with hitting, kicking, gouging or otherwise *harmful contact* with the person. It requires physical contact between the parties.

Criminal assault and battery brings a new issue to bear—namely, whether your hands and feet can be considered deadly weapons. American courts are split on this subject. Numerous defendants have been charged with *aggravated* assault (an offense with greater consequences than simple assault) for injuring others with their bare hands or feet. This contrasts with the norm, where aggravated assault usually refers to assaults with inanimate objects such as pipes or knives.

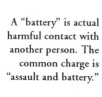

A "battery" is actual harmful contact with another person. The common charge is "assault and battery."

   Courts disagree on whether an assault with bare hands can be considered aggravated assault. Some courts have rejected labeling bare hands as dangerous or deadly weapons. The New York Appeals Court, for example, reversed a first-degree manslaughter conviction, holding "when the legislature talks of a 'dangerous weapon,' it means something quite different from the bare fist of an *ordinary* man" (author's emphasis). In a similar case, *State v. Calvin,* the Louisiana Supreme Court conceded that bare hands are capable of producing "death or great bodily harm," but nevertheless held that "there must be proof of the use of some inanimate object before a defendant can be held guilty of assault 'with a dangerous weapon.'" Many other courts have ruled that mere use of the hands does not constitute aggravated assault. Other courts, however, have been less definite and have held that bare hands may under certain circumstances be considered "dangerous weapons." Therefore, the manner in which your hands and feet are used may be a determining factor.

Most cases in which one is charged with aggravated assault with bare hands usually deal with assault with both the hands *and* feet. Without considering the added factor of footwear (shoes, boots, spike heels, etc.), there are several cases that have held that an assault with hands and feet is not assault with a deadly weapon. The landmark

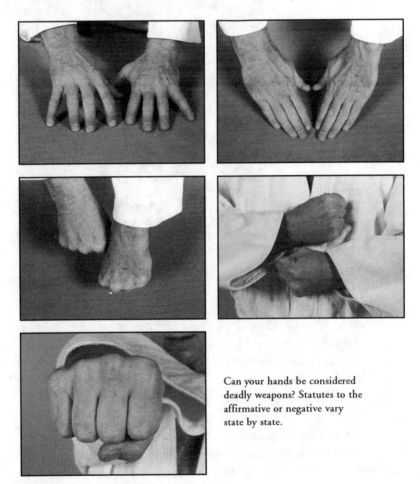

Can your hands be considered deadly weapons? Statutes to the affirmative or negative vary state by state.

case *Wilson v. State* was decided by the Arkansas Supreme Court in 1924. The defendant had beaten and kicked a physician "in the face and side." At his trial the defendant was convicted of assault with a deadly weapon. The Arkansas Supreme Court later modified the charge to simple assault and battery because the defendant used *only* hands and feet. Therefore, "no deadly weapon was used."

With language that many courts have since adopted, the Arkansas Supreme Court argued that capacity to kill is not the same thing as "assault with a deadly weapon," even though the defendant has an unusual ability to fight with his hands and feet:

A powerful man—a Dempsey or Firpo—might kill one by striking with the fist or kicking with the foot, but a great bodily injury by these means would not be an assault with a deadly weapon, instrument, or other thing, in the sense of the aggravated assault statute.

Some commentators have criticized restricting the "deadly/dangerous" weapon label to inanimate objects. Instead of looking to the *object employed,* courts have been urged to take into account the *potential danger of the method used.* This means that the "deadly/dangerous" weapon test should include not just guns or knives, but teeth, fists, a guard dog, or any other animate or inanimate object. For example, if only an inanimate object can be dangerous, then the defendant who pokes out the victim's eye with a finger pays the penalty for simple battery while the co-defendant who pokes out the victim's other eye with a pencil pays the penalty for an aggravated battery.

Other courts, by contrast, have considered the surrounding circumstances and manner in which the instrument was employed. There are several notable cases in which the defendant's hands and/or feet committed the criminal attack. In cases where hands or fists have been used to inflict death or injury, some courts have held the defendants liable under aggravated assault and homicide statutes.

One of the most important cases is *Commonwealth v. Buzard,* decided by the Pennsylvania Supreme Court in 1950. In this case, the court affirmed the defendant's conviction of second-degree murder. The defendant and the victim argued over a $31 lumber bill. This led to a brawl, and the defendant killed the man by straddling him and beating him with blows to the head with his fists. The defendant was taller than the victim by a full six inches and outweighed him by more than 40 pounds. In upholding the defendant's conviction, the Pennsylvania Supreme Court observed:

Fists, though not ordinarily a deadly weapon, may become deadly by repeated and continued blows applied to vital and delicate parts of the body of the defenseless, unresisting victim.

The Pennsylvania Supreme Court thus isolated two elements which could turn fists into deadly weapons: "repeated and continued blows" and administration of these blows to "vital and delicate parts of the body" (a third, lesser element could be found in a "defenseless, unresisting victim"). In *Quarles v. State,* the Georgia Appeals Court held that the jury could consider fists to be deadly weapons, "depending on the manner and means of their use, the wounds inflicted, etc." The court refused to hold as a matter of law that fists were *not* deadly weapons. In *People v. Score,* the California Appeals Court expanded this concept of "special use" while upholding a conviction of assault by means or force likely to produce great bodily harm. The court noted that a proper list of elements for jury consideration would include "the force of the impact, the manner in which (the fist) was used, and the circumstances under which the force was applied."

These examples reveal the analytical approach courts take when determining if the defendant's hands were used to commit second-degree murder or aggravated assault. Apart from the question of footwear (inanimate weapon), courts view the use of feet similarly to the way they view the use of hands in producing a criminal assault. In *State v. Johnson,* decided by the Missouri Supreme Court in 1927, the drunken defendant was found smacking and "kinda stamping" on his wife as he sat on the edge of a boat and she lay in muddy water. The court held that, while the state proved the defendant's guilt of common assault, it had failed to prove the defendant's guilt of assault with felonious intent. However, the court also observed that a felonious assault "could be committed by a strong man *viciously kicking* another in the *head or in some vital part of the body* with feet encased in heavy shoes or boots" (author's emphasis).

The third setting, in which the defendant used both hands and feet to assault the victim, is the most common. When hands and feet combine to assault a victim, it is generally held that they may become deadly weapons "when used in such manner and in such circumstances as are reasonably calculated to produce death." Five cases shed light on these "manner and circumstances." First, *Lyon v. Commonwealth* brought to the attention of the Kentucky Court of Appeals a case where the defendant beat and kicked his elderly (over 65 years old), 135-pound father-in-law for insulting him and shaking a fist in the defendant's face. After examining indictments in cases of this nature, the court instructed that:

If the instrument alleged to have been used is less formidable and deadly than the ordinary things with which homicide is generally produced, then the indictment should aver that the said intrumentality used by the defendant was a deadly weapon when employed by him in a way and manner set forth in the indictment.

Some 26 years later the Kentucky Court of Appeals, hearing *Vogg v. Commonwealth,* cited that ruling to show the judicial inconsistency in this area of the law. The court affirmed the defendant's conviction for "assault with a deadly weapon with intent to kill"—the defendant prisoner had grabbed the jailer "like they teach in the army" (where the defendant formerly had served as a paratrooper), threw the jailer to the ground, then beat and kicked him. The jailer was so badly injured that his doctor "for two hours or more...believed the man had died." Confronted with the facts, the Kentucky Court of Appeals, apparently ignoring Kentucky precedent to the contrary, held "hands and feet...are to be regarded as within the term 'deadly weapon' only when used in such manner and in such circumstances as are reasonably calculated to produce death." To these elements of "manner" and "circumstances reasonably calculated to produce death," the Minnesota Supreme Court in its 1968 *State v. Born* decision added the express consideration (implicit in the Vogg opinion) of *extent of injuries.* In this controversy, the defendant approached his victim in a laundry, shook and pushed him, pursued him, and knocked him down, then brutally kicked him as he lay on the floor "without effective means of defense." The court was faced with the question of whether such an attack was an assault covered under Minnesota Statutes, making criminal "assault with a dangerous weapon but without intent to inflict great bodily harm." To support the inference that the defendant not only wore shoes, but also "used his feet and fists in such a way as to make these appendages dangerous weapons," the court looked, among other things, to "the nature of the injuries sustained by the victim." In accord is *State v. Golladay,* which will be discussed in detail later, where the murder victim's bodily injuries provided the vehicle through which the state introduced evidence of the defendant's training in karate and *jujitsu.*

To complete this analysis, *Pulliam v. State,* decided by the Mississippi Supreme Court in 1974, contributes the element of *force* to the list of elements courts use to decide whether hands and feet are deadly/dangerous weapons. Following an accident, the defendant dragged the victim from his truck, and (according to the victim) knocked him to the ground, then started kicking him in the face and chest. The victim suffered two broken ribs and multiple facial lacerations. The court reversed and sent back the defendant's conviction, noting that it was a reversible error for the trial judge to instruct the jury that hands and feet are deadly weapons. The Mississippi Supreme Court remarked: "While the use of feet and fists ordinarily would not constitute the use of a deadly weapon, they can constitute a deadly weapon if used with *means or force likely to produce death"* (author's emphasis).

"Special Use" of Hands and Feet

In each of the discussed factual situations—the defendant's use of hands, the defendant's use of feet, and the defendant's use of hands and feet—the courts—consciously or not—dealt with issues of "special use." This justified prosecuting the various defendants under aggravated assault (and homicide) statutes since the nature or extent of the assaults were extreme. In the majority of cases, the "special use of hands and feet" meant the assault was vicious or callous. "Special," however, also implies something else: trained, skilled, and experienced use of the hands and feet as assault weapons. It is this dimension of "special" that this book addresses.

Courts look to the "special" use of the hands and feet of skilled fighters when deciding whether their hands or feet are deadly weapons within the meaning of aggravated assault statutes. No doubt the Kentucky Court of Appeals was influenced to disregard prior case law by the Vogg defendant's use of fighting skills to down the jailer. Likewise, the Iowa Supreme Court in *State v. Broten* upheld as relevant the prosecutor's line of questioning that brought out the defendant's record as a Golden Glove boxer. The victim made the fatal mistake of propositioning the defendant's wife. The defendant immediately confronted the victim outside the restaurant. Thereupon, according to the defendant, the victim pushed him. The defendant countered with a left hook that sent the victim crashing to the sidewalk, where he struck his head and died. The Iowa court affirmed the conviction of manslaughter.

In *State v. Golladay*, the Washington Supreme Court reviewed the defendant's first-degree murder conviction. Evidence of the defendant's training in karate and jujitsu was shown at the trial. The murder victim's body was marred with heavy bruises on the hands (presumedly caused by defensive actions), along with other facial, thigh and breast wounds. Certain wounds to the head caused extensive hemorrhaging, resulting in the victim's death. According to the pathologist, "the blows were made with a blunt instrument having a rounded surface." Although the court reversed the conviction on other grounds, it nevertheless held that it was not an error to admit evidence of the defendant's special training in the martial arts:

The defendant next urges that the trial court erred in permitting evidence of defendant's training in karate or jujitsu. It is argued that this evidence could only serve to inflame the minds of the jury. This evidence, however, dealt with the physical ability of defendant to inflict the extensive wounds suffered by the victim, some of which being described as defense wounds. The slight prejudice which may have resulted from this evidence did not outweigh its relevancy. There was no abuse of discretion in this matter.

Aggravated Assaults

The following sections deal with the three ways in which statutes refer to aggravated assaults: assault with a deadly weapon, assault with a dangerous weapon, and assault by means or force likely to cause great bodily injury. The first two sections discuss the shoe as a deadly or dangerous weapon. The third section addresses hands *and* feet as instruments capable of inflicting great bodily injury.

If the defendant employed a deadly weapon, the assault is considered "aggravated." "Deadly weapon" has been variously defined. In *Acres v. United States,* the U.S. Supreme Court defined it as "a thing with which death can be easily and readily produced." Also, the deadliness of a weapon will be found where "great or serious injury is like-

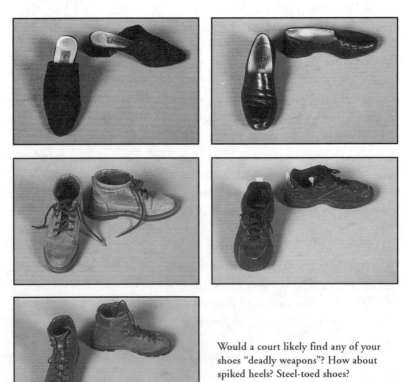

Would a court likely find any of your shoes "deadly weapons"? How about spiked heels? Steel-toed shoes?

ly to result." This raises an inquiry of how shoes might be characterized as deadly weapons. This goes to statutory construction, where courts strictly construe the phrase "deadly weapons." Shoes don't fall within the scope of the statute.

There exists a split of legal authority regarding whether a shoe can ever constitute a deadly weapon as defined by aggravated assault statutes. The majority view holds that under certain circumstances, it can. Still, some courts strictly construe aggravated assault statutes and hold that ordinary shoes are not deadly weapons. In *Dickson v. State,* the Arkansas Supreme Court affirmed the aggravated assault conviction of a defendant who had beaten and kicked the mayor, causing brain damage and a ruptured eardrum. Although testimony established no more than that the mayor was struck with the defendant's hands and shoed feet, the court nevertheless sustained the jury's finding that a deadly weapon was used. Testimony established that the defendant had a pistol at some point before the assault and had time to dispose of it after the assault. The court apparently preferred to infer a pistol-whipping rather than wrestle with the legal questions raised by a finding that the injuries resulted from kicks. This inference was necessary to affirm the conviction since the court noted, "the shoes which a person wears as a part of his ordinary apparel are not deadly weapons, within the meaning of the statute relative to aggravated assault."

The majority of courts hold that shoes can be deadly weapons as defined by aggravated assault statutes. Numerous factors are considered. Since the "deadly character" is a by-product of "the manner and circumstances" in which the shoes are used, the question becomes one of fact for the jury. And since shoes are not inherently deadly, the question for the jury to decide is whether a shoe "assumes the characteristics of a deadly weapon." The Colorado Supreme Court in *Grass v. People* considered the following elements significant in deciding whether a shoe is a deadly weapon: "The nature of the instrument or thing, the manner of its use, the location on the body of the injuries inflicted and the extent of such injuries."

In *Bass v. State,* the Florida court elaborated on "the nature of the instrument or thing." There, the defendant appealed his conviction of assault with a deadly weapon on the grounds that since the assault was committed using only the fists and feet, it could not constitute assault with a deadly weapon within the meaning of the applicable statute. The court distinguished between fists and feet (shoed), noting that there may be some merit to the defendant's argument regarding fists "but the same cannot be said for the contention that shoes do not constitute a deadly weapon." The court laid great stress on the particular characteristics of the shoes worn by the defendant at the time of the assault. In an oft-quoted passage, the court observed:

Shoes come in all shapes, sizes, forms and materials—from the delicate creations of silk and leather, or satin and plastic, to the cleated, hobnailed, iron-toed, leather-heeled boots of the cowboy—any one of which may be capable of inflicting grievous bodily harm or death. The records of medical science are replete with case histories of persons being seriously wounded or killed after being struck by the high heel of a woman's shoe, or having the "boot put to him" by a strong man. It is a jury question as to whether or not a shoe or boot constitutes a deadly weapon, under all the circumstances surrounding the shoe or boot, its size, weight and construction, and the manner in which it was used.

Philosophy of the Courts

The extremes to which courts may go in this philosophy is seen in *Johnson v. State,* a 1971 Florida decision. The court conceded that a shoe could be a deadly weapon, but it reversed the defendant's "aggravated assault with a deadly weapon" conviction since "there was no evidence whatsoever that a shoe was involved."

A second aggravated assault is assault with a *dangerous* weapon. Differentiation between a "deadly" weapon and a "dangerous" weapon is more semantic than real. In some cases, it represents a casual word choice more than a policy of gradating offenses. However, since in the minds of some courts the deadly/dangerous dichotomy represents a difference in degree, separate treatment is justified.

As with "deadly weapons," the concept of "dangerous weapon" entails the capacity to inflict serious injuries. As the District Court for Delaware noted in *United States v. Barber* with respect to shoes, "Almost any object 'which as used or attempted to be used may endanger life or inflict great bodily harm' or (that) which 'is likely to produce death or great bodily injury' can in certain circumstances be a dangerous weapon."

In determining whether a dangerous weapon was used, courts look to both the use and the nature of the defendant's footgear. Regarding use, *Smith v. State,* decided by the Oklahoma Criminal Court of Appeals, lends guidance. There the court heard an appeal from a conviction for assault with a dangerous weapon. The defendant had been prosecuted for hitting and kicking (with heavy shoes) an elderly woman. Since the court found no evidence that *kicking* caused the injury, the conviction was affirmed only as assault and battery. However, the court observed that shoes are not dangerous weapons per se, but can become such "by their manner of use...under certain circumstances." The Iowa Supreme Court in *State v. Bradley,* the District Court for Delaware in *United States v. Barber,* and the D.C. Circuit in *Medlin v. United States* are in accord.

Regarding the nature of the footgear, the majority and dissenting opinions in *Ransom v. State* provide an excellent discussion. In essence, the Alaska Supreme Court overturned the defendant's conviction because the state proved merely that the victim was assaulted with "footgear," not with "boots." The majority used the following analysis to reach its conclusion that the conviction must be overturned:

(We cannot) conclude that the variance between "boots" and "footgear" is immaterial. It is true that many kinds of shoes could be considered the rough equivalent of boots. However,...one of the questions the jury was to answer was whether the "boots" of Ransom were dangerous weapons. Because of this required determination, the physical characteristics of Ransom's footgear cannot be considered immaterial. The term "footgear" could include such a variety of shoes, sandals, slippers and mukluks besides boots that we cannot see how a jury could reasonably decide whether Ransom's "footgear" was a dangerous weapon.

Concurring in part and dissenting in part, the judge raised a fresh consideration. His contention was that the use of the footgear as "instruments of offensive combat," not whether the footgear was boots or shoes, should largely determine whether an assault with footgear was an assault with a deadly weapon.

Consideration of cases dealing with striking or kicking as assault, by means or force likely to cause great bodily harm, concludes this aggravated assault offense discussion. These cases differ from the others previously discussed in two respects. First, the emphasis shifts from instrumentalities to manner. (This is implicit in the statement of the offense and does not depend on judicial construction for its existence.) Second, using *both* hands and feet as a means of inflicting great bodily harm will be discussed.

The felonious assault created when one hits or kicks with force, or means likely to cause great bodily harm, need not be carried out with a deadly weapon to fall within the scope of aggravated assault. It seems clear that the amount of force, not whether an object is used, is the relevant inquiry. For the offense to exist, it is not necessary, quoting the colorful language of a California opinion, "that the victim be held over a blazing furnace or be fired upon with an atomic weapon;" a hit or kick may suffice. The nature and extent of the victim's injuries are relevant and may help determine whether the force was of a felonious character.

Kicking a person in the face and head, for example, has been found to enter the scope of aggravated assault. Unfortunately, some courts still look to the character of the shoes, even when the prosecution is for assault by means or force likely to cause great bodily harm.

Fists also enter the scope of aggravated assault. They may be used as "a force likely to produce death or great bodily harm" whether or not a deadly weapon is involved. In at least one case, *People v. Zankich,* the defendant's closed fist was shown to the jury so they could determine whether it seemed capable of inflicting serious bodily injury. The relevant inquiry is the degree of force utilized by the defendant. In *People v. Fuentes,* the California Appeals Court held that a knockout punch to the jaw was not a blow sufficiently powerful to be viewed as a blow likely to cause great bodily injury. That view has subsequently met with disapproval.

The Martial Artists

Before going on to "lessons for the trained fighter," some discussion of the fighting arts and the special ability trained fighters enjoy is needed.

Martial artists, of course, have special fighting abilities—their entire bodies have been transformed into veritable fighting machines. They manifest their abilities in various ways. *Karateka* and kung fu practitioners strike with their hands and kick with their feet. Judo, *aikido* and jujitsu practitioners stress throwing, choking, holding and arm-locking techniques. Judo and jujitsu also contain striking techniques *(atemi waza)*. For present purposes, the striking and kicking techniques of martial artists will be emphasized.

The hands and feet of trained martial artists are flesh-and-blood weapons which can easily inflict injuries comparable to those inflicted by a club or knife. In fact, persons have died at the hands (and feet) of martial artists. For analytical purposes, an examination of this "capacity for destruction" enjoyed by martial artists will focus on three elements: deliberate toughening of the hands and feet, skilled or special use of the hands and feet, and conscious "targeting" of strikes and kicks. To envision these three elements operating in unison, the reader should envision a karateka hurling a hard, toughened fist at some pressure point on the opponent's body. In practice, it is uncommon for any one martial art to lay equal emphasis on all three elements. For example, while judoka do not condition their hands, martial artists that practice certain styles of karate

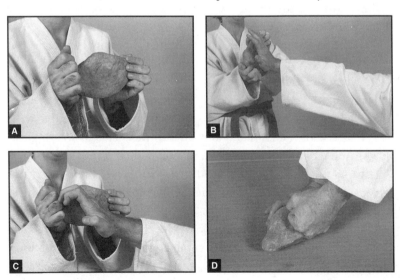

(a) A smooth river rock is the ultimate makiwara board. With it, you can toughen the heel, side and knuckles of your hands, (b, c and d).

A properly executed corkscrew punch can be one of the most powerful
and useful weapons in your fighting arsenal. (1) From a

toughen their hands and feet. Jujitsu and kung fu exalt *targeted*
blows over *powerful* blows. All striking techniques, however, share
the element of "skilled or special use." Each of the mentioned martial arts teaches the proper way to kick or strike to maximize the
damage inflicted.

The first component of a martial artist's personal "capacity for
destruction" is the conditioning of his hands or feet to harden the
skin where impact occurs. This practice prevails in kung fu and
certain karate styles. Toughening the hands has traditionally been
achieved on a *makiwara* board. Martial artists repeatedly strike
this board with the knuckles and sides of their hands, creating cal-
luses. Additionally, some karateka harden their hands and fingers
by sifting them through boxes filled with sand, then rice, then
gravel. Kung fu masters toughen their hands by soaking them in
vats of herb juices.

This is one karateka's routine: Twice a day he struck his *dojo's*
concrete walls 300 times "with enough power to knock out most
men." He concluded the ritual by cutting deep grooves into the sides
and first two knuckles of each hand (points of contact for chops and
blows) with razor blades and plunging the blood-spurting hand into

front horse stance, (2) release your right fist and set it spinning,
(3) resulting in a strong punch, (a) (close up).

a white mud mixture made of salt and water.

To condition his hands, Mas Oyama, one of modern karate's fathers, would go to the mountains each winter and camp beside a healthy pine tree. Every morning he would pound the tree 200 consecutive times. When the tree died, Oyama took it as a sign to break camp and leave the mountains.

Bare feet are conditioned similarly. Karateka Ronnie Barkoot conditioned his feet by running, barefooted, to the top of Atlanta's steep and craggy Stone Mountain, then back down again. When the bare soles hit the sharp rocks, the weight and pressure would pop the skin open, much like a dart hitting a water balloon. Nerves and muscles hung on the bottom, and some of the toes resembled bloody-red cauliflowers.

The second component is the force and manner with which a martial artist administers blows and kicks. The manner fuels the force. By *snapping* punches and kicks (returning the fist or foot to its point of departure), a martial artist multiplies the velocity—and therefore power—of the blow or kick. This quick recoil also removes the foot or fist from the opponent's clutches.

Kicks are more powerful than hand blows. However, strikes

An example of a "targeted blow"—(1) focus on the target (your adversary's knee) and (2) advance forward by bringing your left leg

with the hand of a skilled martial artist can also be devastating. In killing a healthy bull with his bare hands, Mas Oyama undoubtedly gave the single-most spectacular and decisive display of punching power in martial arts history. Before motion picture cameras, Oyama provoked the bull with well-aimed pebbles, then ran, prompting the beast to give pursuit. Moments before the bull made contact, Oyama twirled and lobbed off a horn with his bare hands. He then battered the bull with deadly blows until it fell to the ground in a lifeless heap. The butcher who carted the dead creature away later claimed that the blows rendered the bull unfit for human consumption.

Martial artists are not limited to striking with the hands and feet. Some break 300-pound blocks of ice with their heads. Similar feats have been performed with elbows and knees.

The third component is the deliberate targeting of kicks and blows. Most prevalent in jujitsu and kung fu, this "targeting" is likewise relevant to non-striking, non-kicking techniques. For example, judo and jujitsu experts apply chokes and armlocks to specific parts of the body to maximize strangulation and joint impairment. Judo and aikido adepts throw opponents by avoiding their opponents, then heaving.

in a counterclockwise loop, then (3) lift and cock your right leg, and (4) execute the blow, striking your adversary's right knee cap.

As one college judo instructor pointed out, "Bullies don't have the mentality to learn (judo) because they don't have the patience; they want something quick and easy, and it takes two to three years to do good judo." Some martial arts instructors refuse to teach students who show signs of misusing their knowledge.

Nevertheless, martial artists have committed aggravated assaults. In Pittsburgh, a police officer was injured by a karate-trained suspect. Recently, a mother was sentenced to prison for complicity in the death by beating of her two-year-old daughter. She made no attempt to stop her boyfriend and children from practicing karate blows on the two-year-old child.

In determining whether the hands and feet of martial artists are aggravated assault weapons, it is useful to refer to a 1968 survey. Twenty-six law enforcement agencies were queried whether the use of karate would constitute an aggravated crime, such as assault with a deadly weapon. Nine responses were categorical affirmatives. Eleven other responses indicated that an "assault with a deadly weapon" prosecution *could* be successful, depending on the circumstances.

Under certain circumstances, criminal assaults by unarmed martial artists *should* be treated as aggravated assaults. Quite simply, the hands and feet of martial artists *can* be dangerous weapons,

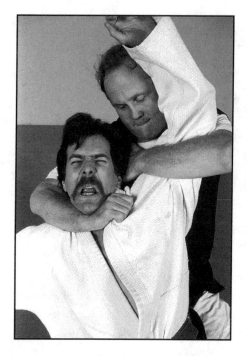

Another example of a "targeted blow" is the choke, such as the *okuri eri jime* choke pictured here. A *judoka* targets his opponent by placing simultaneous pressure on the back of his opponent's head with the back of his left hand while pulling his right arm across his neck like a noose.

and can cause great bodily harm. Implicit in many opinions holding that hands and feet are not deadly or dangerous weapons is the *Vollmer* court notion (i.e., aggravated assault legislation envisions the "ordinary man" as its potential defendant). Given this assumption, it is reasonable to require the presence of inanimate weapons before prosecuting this ordinary man for aggravated assault. One who by virtue of special training can employ his or her hands and feet as deadly weapons graduates from "ordinary man" status and should be treated no differently from the knife- or club-wielder. It is the *result* (serious harm to the victim) or its potential (not whether an animate of inanimate object inflicted that harm) that underpins and justifies aggravated assault statutes. Therefore, it seems that the Arkansas Supreme Court was mistaken when it remarked in its *Wilson* opinion that a blow from Jack Dempsey would not be an assault with a deadly weapon. A blow from Dempsey, or a side-thrust kick from a skilled karateka, should be considered as no less deadly or dangerous than an inept club assault from some hoodlum.

In deciding whether the hands and feet of martial artists were, in fact, employed as aggravated assault weapons, several facts should be determined. Five of the considerations or elements find support in current case law:

—the nature of the injuries received by the victim;
—the force used by the defendant;
—whether repeated blows were struck;
—the manner or style of attack;
—and whether the blows and kicks were administered to vital areas of the victim's body.

When the defendant is a martial artist, at least two more inquiries should be raised. First, whether the defendant has had special training as a fighter, and the extent of such training, should be determined. The importance of this inquiry has been implicitly or explicitly recognized in the *Golladay, Vogg, Broten* and *Bean* opinions where the criminal defendants were, respectively, a karateka, ex-paratrooper, and two boxers. The defendant's skill as a martial artist is important in determining if the assault was deadly, dangerous, or likely to cause great injury. After all, disproportionate power, not just dangers of attack by the use of inanimate objects, is the ultimate danger against which aggravated assault statutes are designed.

Two considerations qualify this inquiry into special skill. First, courts should distinguish among martial artists. All other things being equal, the martial arts *expert* could and should more readily be found guilty of aggravated assault than the *novice* martial artist. It is only the expert who can wield hands and feet as dangerous or deadly weapons. In measuring expertise, courts will find belt ranks a convenient yardstick. The professionally taught expert should be distinguished from the self-taught/paperback-taught "expert." Those falling in the latter category possess no true or unique skill and should be treated the same as non-martial artists.

A second inquiry should be made about the condition of the martial artist's hands and feet. As discussed earlier, many martial artists deliberately condition their hands and feet to transform them into clublike weapons. Many of the same considerations courts have given to the weight, size, texture, etc., of a shoe could logically apply to the *bare* hands or *bare* feet of a martial artist. Authority already exists for showing the defendant's fist to the jury, like an exhibit, to illustrate its weapon-like character.

When martial artists are prosecuted for aggravated assault, the presence or absence of shoes loses relevance. While it may be true that shoes enhance the ability of laypersons to inflict injury, the opposite is often true for martial artists. Martial artists train barefooted, kicking with the ball, heel and side of the foot. Kicks are faster and more accurately targeted when delivered shoeless. Moreover, kicks to the face and flying kicks are easier to execute when barefooted. Bare feet of karate-ka are often more dangerous than the booted feet of laypersons. Therefore, the *Johnson* extreme, where the state's failure to prove the defendant wore shoes resulted in a reversal of the defendant's conviction for assault with a deadly weapon, isn't logical if applied to martial artists. There are martial artists whose first impulse in street encounters is to kick off shoes to improve their kicking techniques. The Alaska Supreme Court justice was on the right track when he argued that the *kind of footgear* employed was a secondary consideration compared with the matter of whether the feet were used as "instruments of offensive combat."

The danger is that martial artists will be perfunctorily prosecuted for aggravated assaults when the evidence might call for a simple assault prosecution. Martial artists can "pull" punches and kicks, lessening their impact. They can use non-deadly techniques. And they can simply use non-martial arts modes of fighting. Therefore, while martial artists are deadly fighters, it would be unfair to assume that their hands and feet were used as deadly or dangerous weapons, unless the evidence supports such a finding.

Apart from the judicial determination that hands or feet were used as deadly weapons, attention must be given to regulatory legislation. There exists a popular American belief that martial artists must register their hands as deadly weapons with the police department.

Whatever the source of this "modern myth," its survival and propagation has been aided by uninformed martial artists as well as uninformed laypersons. A 1968 survey categorically and unequivocally denied that karateka had to "register their hands as deadly weapons." This, of course, begs the real question—is such registration desirable?

While it is true that few, if any, legal restrictions are uniquely imposed on martial artists, this writer nevertheless feels "registration" affords no solution. In the first place, the enforcement problem would be staggering. Should law enforcement officers be successful in securing registration of the untold thousands of martial artists who have received professional instruction, this leaves unregistered an invisible mass of "martial artists" who have had no formal instruction. While these paperback-martial artists are less dangerous, they are far more likely to become criminal defendants. A second problem exists in the logical inconsistency posed by registering martial artists. Pocketknife wielders have similar abilities to harm others (though perhaps to a lesser degree). Pocketknife wielders, in fact, may pose a greater social danger than martial artists since martial artists are prone to avoid all street encounters by virtue of their training. Third, and last, no vital state interest would be served by registration of martial artists. This can be contrasted with registering firearms. To some, registration of firearms makes sense because lost or stolen firearms can be used by others to commit crimes. Firearm registration provides names, leading to suspects. Registration of martial artists would serve no similar purposes. The hands and feet of martial artists cannot be used by others. Severe injuries can be inflicted by large, untrained men, or small men with bludgeons. Registration isn't a cure-all.

CHAPTER THREE

Martial Arts and the Presumption of Deadly Ability

For good or evil, martial artists are regarded by some as deadly fighters. This reputation is true in some cases, but it is usually undeserved or exaggerated. The attrition rate in the martial arts is notoriously high—well over 90 percent, over time. Most students drop out of the martial arts altogether, for less demanding alternatives, before they reach black belt. Furthermore, those who practice martial arts long enough to acquire good fighting skills are usually the last to injure others. Black belts are the first to walk away from mayhem. The great catch-22 is that while most people enter the martial arts to learn how to fight, once they truly become proficient as fighters they are chary to use their fighting skills unless backed into a wall.

With the exception of the television series *Kung Fu,* however, this is not always the popular viewpoint. The image of martial artists is molded by television and movies. If Chuck Norris is involved in a fight, it will sometimes have a predictable end. Deadly force and crushing blows are expected to thunder from the trained fighter. The spirit of Bruce Lee somehow lives in all martial artists.

This has serious consequences for a martial artist if his or her knowledge of, or training in, the martial arts is brought out at trial. In some cases, it is probative and should be admitted. In other cases, it is quite the contrary. Decide for yourself if justice is served in each of the following court cases.

Presumption of Martial Artists' Deadly Ability to Inflict Injury

First is the case of *People v. Dabney.* The defendant was convicted of rape and sexual abuse, both in the first degree, and appealed. Among other alleged errors at trial, he claimed it was prejudicial to allow testimony of his familiarity with karate.

The appellate court held that "(l)imited testimony given by a YMCA supervisor, who had observed defendant practice Karate, was probative of defendant's actual knowledge of Karate; as such, the testimony was relevant and admissible to establish a factual predicate for the complainant's asserted fear of the defendant's use of force against her."

Interestingly, the only physical injury to the rape victim that was noted on appeal was a scratch to her neck. This was hardly a "karate-based injury," yet evidence about the defendant's martial arts training was nevertheless allowed by the court. This case was overturned on appeal, *infra* (discussed later).

Next is the case of *People v. Corbett*. Winfield Proffitt and a friend wanted to score some weed, and they asked two strangers where they could buy marijuana. They were led to a park, where Proffitt and the defendant Michael Corbett entered to supposedly make the purchase. Shortly thereafter, Proffitt staggered to the porch of a nearby house where he fell dead, mortally wounded by a knife wound six to 10 inches in depth. Defendant Corbett was convicted of first-degree murder and appealed.

One of the grounds for appeal was that testimony about his skill in the martial arts was irrelevant and highly prejudicial in that it showed a predilection for violence.

The appellate court disagreed. The testimony consisted of an explanation of Corbett's skills in two basic areas of the martial arts. In the words of the court:

One category involved the use of various body movements and the other concerned the use of swords and knives. The testimony about defendant's ability in the martial arts involving body movements may have been irrelevant as the victim died not from a surface blow to the body, but from a stab wound. However, it was an integral part of the testimony of one witness concerning the types of martial arts in which the defendant had engaged, the instruction he had received, and the competitions in which he had participated. The testimony of defendant's skill with knives was relevant to show his familiarity with knives and ability to manipulate them, even though the evidence did not indicate that the victim had been stabbed in any unusual manner which was indicative of martial arts training. The issue once more is whether the prejudicial effect of the evidence outweighed its probative value.

The court went on to say the evidence was not presented in an inflammatory manner and that there was no indication the defendant had ever misused his skills. The trial court had instructed the jury that the evidence was offered "only for the limited purpose of showing the physical accomplishments of the defendant in the martial arts sports and it was not to be considered as a reflection on the defendant's character."

I think this was a terrible decision. Anyone can slash another with a knife; this "skill" is not limited to martial artists. It is ironic that karate means "empty hands" fighting.

Another case where karate training was allowed in the record is *State v. McNish.* Defendant McNish was convicted of murder in the first degree and was sentenced to death by electrocution. As you might expect, McNish appealed. His victim was a frail, elderly lady who was 70 years old and weighed less than 100 pounds. McNish "weighed about 165 pounds and *held a black belt in karate*" (author's emphasis). The appellate court noted "Mrs. Smith was mercilessly beaten to death by repeated blows by an assailant who was obviously much more powerful than she was."

There was no discussion on appeal about the defendant having a black belt in karate. It was likely not raised as a separate issue and may not even have been objected to at trial. In any event, it does not seem relevant and was likely prejudicial. It certainly does not take a black belt to beat a 70-year-old woman to death with a vase, or even with bare hands. The defendant, no doubt, got what he deserved (the verdict and sentence were affirmed), but the martial arts got another black eye—which it did not deserve.

Another case wherein evidence of martial arts experience was questionably admitted at trial is *State v. O'Connell.* Here, defendant Thomas O'Connell was convicted of second-degree murder of his wife and eight-month-old daughter. The bodies of the victims were found in their burning mobile home. The mother died of strangulation before the fire was set, and the baby daughter died of smoke inhalation.

On appeal, the defendant through counsel asserted that his karate *(tae kwon do) gi* should not have been allowed into evidence at trial. The State, without objection, had entered the gi into evidence. It further presented testimony that the green belt indicated a lower to middle proficiency in the martial art. The trial attorney objected to this on grounds of relevancy and was overruled. The appellate court noted:

A green belt like the one shown here was entered into evidence in the case *State V. O'Connell.* The appellate court held "The evidence tended to prove defendant possessed the capacity to inflict the injuries disclosed by the autopsy."

The autopsy conducted on Carole (the deceased wife) disclosed she suffered abrasions on both the left and right side of her neck. The hyoid bone in her neck was broken. There were bruises on the inside of her mouth, left side of her face, hip and ribs. There were hemorrhages in the right ear areas. The doctor testified these injuries were caused by 'blunt force,' consistent with blows struck by a fist or foot.

The appellate court called it a close question, but upheld the lower court, noting that "the evidence tended to prove defendant possessed the capacity to inflict the injuries disclosed by the autopsy."

Yes, a green belt in tae kwon do could inflict the injuries sustained by the defendant's wife. So too could a layman. Men kill their wives every day and it does not take martial arts training to do so.

Next are cases wherein the threatened use of martial arts was used to rape and rob. In each instance, the court found the victim's fear justifiable and upheld the defendant's conviction. First is the case of *People v. Ward.* Defendant Albert Ward was convicted of repeatedly raping his stepdaughter. The 14-year-old was coerced by Ward's threats of "taking out" her mother. The threats were taken seriously, in part, because Ward "frequently demonstrated his interest and skill in the martial arts. He boasted...about the many ways he knew of killing a person." The court reasoned, "The law protects against unfounded charges by its requirement that the victim act upon an objectively reasonable basis in concluding there is a possibility the perpetrator will execute the threat if the victim does not submit." In this case, the court noted "(T)he girl knew her stepfather was a convicted murderer. He also spoke frequently to her of killing people. He demonstrated to the girl numerous ways, using martial arts, to kill a person." Ward's lawyer, on appeal, conceded, "In appellant's case, there is no doubt that he possessed the ability to carry out his threats..."

In Ward's case, the presumption of "deadly ability" was well-deserved and properly within the scope of the appellate record.

Another case where a martial artist threatened mayhem to effectuate rape is *Williams v. State*. Williams told his victim "he had a black belt in karate," then "demonstrated what he could do to her with his karate expertise"; he even threatened her daughter. Again, this is a case where the defendant's martial arts abilities were properly put into evidence.

In the case of *State v. Morse*, the issue before the Supreme Court of Maine was whether a hold-up victim was threatened with physical harm in the present (robbery) or in the future (extortion). The defendant wanted the crime to be characterized as "theft by extortion" because this carried a lesser sentence. The court reviewed the facts. "While they were (in the victim's apartment) defendant demanded money from Tremblay, after first informing him that he was a karate expert. Tremblay handed over to defendant more than $150, which was in a dresser drawer. Defendant further rifled the dresser, threatened to tie up Tremblay, knocked him to the floor and left." On this evidence, the court concluded:

(D)efendant threatened Tremblay with present physical harm: the immediate use of his presently-existing karate prowess against Tremblay if Tremblay did not act as defendant then wanted him to act. So understanding defendant's threat, Tremblay immediately submitted.

Clearly, this was also a case where admission of martial arts prowess was relevant and germane.

Next is a bizarre case where the *defense attorney* put in proof of his client's deadly fighting ability to prove *had* the defendant attacked the victim, he surely would have killed her! The case is *State v. Jarrell*.

Defendant Jarrell was helping college freshman Capice Bernson change a flat tire in a shopping center parking garage. While she worked on the lug nuts she was struck from behind, without warning, with a tire iron. She testified that Jarrell struck her, and he claimed that someone else struck her while some third party held a gun to his head.

At trial, Jarrell was convicted of attempted criminal homicide.

In a truly novel defense move, Jarrell's attorney during direct examination asked several questions that put the defendant's fighting ability before the jury and into the record.

Defendant revealed that he had participated in clandestine activities for the government of Thailand, that he had trained in the martial arts, and that in the course of his activities he had killed at least six people; one he had killed with his 'bare hands.' The purpose of this direct examination was apparently to support the defense theory that because of his background and skills, had defendant been Ms. Bernson's assailant...he would have killed her.

The conviction was affirmed and the martial artist was hoisted by his own petard.

One appellate court found that admission of martial arts training *was prejudicial.* This is a case already covered, *People v. Dabney.* Remember Dabney? He was the convicted rapist who appealed on the grounds that evidence of his martial arts training was prejudicial. He lost his first appeal, *supra* (earlier discussed), then appealed again to the highest court in the state of New York—the New York Court of Appeals.

In a terse, one-page opinion, the high court reversed the lower appellate court and held that it was prejudicial error "for the trial court to...allow testimony by the YMCA supervisor concerning defendant's practice of karate." This, coupled with the lower court's refusal to admit certain hospital records, led the court to hold that "the combined effect of these erroneous evidentiary determinations, when viewed in conjunction with the trial court's minimal instruction to the jury as to the element of forcible compulsion, was highly prejudicial to the defendant."

The importance of the Dabney case to martial artists and their lawyers cannot be stressed enough. Put a bookmark on this page. This

Handcuffs and ankle manacles have been used to "protect witnesses and courtroom decorum."

case stands for the proposition that courts should not automatically allow evidence of martial arts training into the courtroom when such evidence is irrelevant and prejudicial. While this is only "binding precedence" in New York, it is "persuasive authority" in every other state. Put this with your martial arts weapons and don't forget about it.

Martial Artists In Chains

This book is a testament to the fact that more and more martial artists are finding themselves in the courtroom as civil and criminal defendants. As discussed in the previous section, martial artists often enter the courtroom with a strike against them. They are, after all, *martial artists*—bigger than life, skilled fighters, masters of mayhem with Bruce Lee's spirit coursing through their veins, conquerors of all they survey.

Consequently, fair in some cases and ridiculous in others, martial artists are stigmatized when they walk into a courtroom and the judge allows such a designation into evidence.

Worse still, but understandable in some cases, martial artists who are criminal defendants can be handcuffed and put in shackles (leg manacles). Imagine what impact *that* has on a jury! Here, the "presumption of guilt" hangs heavy.

At least three appellate courts have addressed the matter. First is the case of *Commonwealth v. Montgomery.* Criminal defendant Wayne Montgomery was convicted of unlawfully carrying a firearm and with the unlawful possession of ammunition. A brown belt in karate, Montgomery's legs were shackled at the trial, like some runaway slave, as a "security measure." He was allowed at the counsel table without handcuffs, but despite objection he was required to wear leg shackles, which the jurors saw. The defendant had been accused of an attempted escape and "the court officer had also been told by one of the jail guards that the defendant was a 'brown belt in karate,' a fact which he, the court officer, believed created a risk if no restraints were imposed."

The defendant appealed his conviction, arguing, among other things, that it was prejudicial error to make him wear leg irons in front of the jury, compromising his right to a fair trial. The Appeals Court

Imua kuon tao kung fu
fighting stance

Never fall into a fighting
stance during a confrontation
with a law enforcement
officer. The officer may
misinterpret the stance as
an attack, and respond
accordingly.

Tien sun wushu
fighting stance

of Massachusetts found the leg shackles "troublesome," but nevertheless affirmed the conviction, reasoning:

There was evidence before (the trial judge) that the defendant posed a security risk. The judge forcefully instructed on the presumption of innocence, although the judge did not, as suggested (in a previous case) instruct the jury to draw no inference from the fact that the defendant had leg shackles. The defendant did not seek such an instruction... (T)aking the trial as a whole, there is not sufficient cause to override the judge's exercise of discretion in adopting the safety precautions.

We cannot know how much weight was given to the defendant's "brown belt in karate," but it was obviously important enough to be mentioned in the case. Nowhere does the court discuss that the defendant *used* his martial arts training in an anti-social way.

Again, here we have a defendant with a big MA (martial artist) stamped indelibly on his chest. We have to shrug and resent the baggage a martial artist carries into a courtroom by virtue of being a trained fighter.

Next is the case of *State v. Gilcrist*. Prison inmates Alvin Gilcrist and Kenneth Agtuca were convicted of stabbing a fellow inmate 31 times with knives crafted from broom handles and metal rods. After a bomb exploded outside the courtroom and one of the witnesses threw water on the jury, the prisoners were put "in arm and leg chains and were seated directly behind their attorneys" as a security measure.

The issue of arm and leg chains was raised on appeal, and the Supreme Court of Washington held this did not, under the circumstances, deny the prisoners the right to a fair trial.

(W)e do not believe the use of security measures here violated appellants' right to a fair trial. In this case, Gilcrist gestured obscenely to the court; he and Agtuca delayed their trial by spilling liquids on their clothing; their first witness tossed water on the jury; a number of their other inmate witnesses testified they practiced martial arts within the prison (author's emphasis) *and a bomb exploded outside the courtroom.*

Again, we do not know how much weight was given to the fact that the prisoners practiced martial arts. But it must have had some importance for the court to include it in its appellate opinion. Unlike the *Montgomery* case, however, there appears to be much better reasons in this instance to chain and shackle the murderous defendants in light of their behavior at trial.

Lastly, the case of *Hawaii v. Castro* sheds more light on the question of shackling martial artists in courtrooms. Here, for a change, the court found that the defendant should not have been shackled during trial.

Michael Castro was convicted of attempted murder and assault in the first degree following a jury trial. One of his grounds for appeal was that he was shackled during much of the trial and excluded from the courtroom thereafter.

Castro showed up at the strip bar where his estranged girlfriend worked and "suddenly leaped from his seat, grabbed the woman by her hair, and yelled 'let's go.' He stabbed her repeatedly in the back and neck with a knife as he dragged her toward the door."

At trial, understandably enough, Castro's former girlfriend was afraid to take the stand. The prosecutor moved to have Castro shackled because "the witness...was fearful that Castro would harm her if he could freely move about the courtroom." The trial court granted the motion, over strenuous objection, because "the assault weapon had been placed in evidence and could possibly be reached by the defendant, he had a history of violence, *he was versed in martial arts* (author's emphasis) and he was in an emotional state, as evidenced by his sobbing while prospective jurors were being examined."

The appellate court concluded that Castro should not have been shackled during trial and that such action was "inherently prejudicial" under the circumstances. It held:

But even a partial physical restraint of the accused while he sits before the judge and jury is not to be lightly ordered, for shackling unmistakably indicates 'the need to separate the defendant from the community at large.' And it 'is the sort of inherently prejudicial practice that...should be permitted only where justified by an essential specific to (the) trial.'

A good decision? You decide. Clearly courts can use martial arts prowess—rightly or wrongly—when deciding whether a trained fighter can be shackled in the courtroom.

Cops and Fighting Stances

What happens when a police officer attempts to make an arrest and is confronted with a fighting stance? Three cases address this question.

First is the case of *Fontenot v. Fontenot.* The plaintiff was arrested after a scuffle in the parking lot of a bar (from which he had just been ejected). The police arrived and one officer told the plaintiff to empty his pockets. There the accounts diverge.

The cop testified he told the plaintiff to empty his pockets and the plaintiff responded by "assuming a karate-like stance in defiance of the order."

The plaintiff contended he had a seizure, rendering his left side dysfunctional, and his hand (going after medicine) got stuck in his pocket.

Both sides agreed as to what happened afterward. Two policemen wailed hell out of the plaintiff with their nightsticks.

The plaintiff brought a civil lawsuit against the police. The Court of Appeals of Louisiana found for the plaintiff, although it did not address excessive force. This, nevertheless, is a good case to remember for martial artists in trouble with the law under similar circumstances.

The next case, *State v. Sickler,* came to a more tragic end. "In the early morning hours of July 12, 1981, the Lincoln County Sheriff, Kenneth Albers, responded to a report of a man lying on a road. When Sheriff Albers arrived at the reported location he found appellant, whom he recognized, asleep on the road. The sheriff woke him up, told him to move off the road, and offered him a ride home. Appellant became progressively agitated and angry, refused to leave, and referred to the sheriff as Captain Smith from his war experiences. Sheriff Albers testified he did not consider physical contact with appellant because he knew appellant was a very strong man. He called his deputy, Darrell Nelson, for assistance. Shortly after Nelson arrived, appellant, who was standing two to three feet from the officers, pulled a knife from his clothing. He opened the blade and with knife in hand advanced toward the officers *making karate and sweeping motions* (author's emphasis). The officers backed off and repeatedly ordered appellant to drop the knife, but appellant continued his menacing movements. The sheriff said he feared being stabbed. The sheriff then shot him (in the abdomen)."

The Supreme Court of South Dakota upheld the appellant's conviction of aggravated assault. To compromise the usefulness of this case, the sheriff had several reasons to be afraid of Mr. Sickler—i.e., the knife, the physical strength, and the psychotic allusions to the war (mistaking Sheriff Albers for Captain Smith). The "karate motions" were just part of an intimidating package.

The third case of this trilogy ends the most tragically, in an ultimate suicide. In *District of Columbia v. Peters,* an arrestee who was shot by a police officer, was left paralyzed from the chest down. He brought suit, but he committed suicide before it went to trial. His wife continued the civil action.

Raymond Peters, a soldier, returned home to celebrate Christmas and to face a PCP drug charge. He went to his mother's house and found a mahogany cane he had owned for several years. He smoked PCP with his friend, then left to pick up his wife. She "noticed he was acting strangely; he was driving fast and talking loudly."

After the two arrived at their house, Raymond Peters went outside and "stood in the middle of the street and hit passing cars with his cane." Two drivers got out and tried to disarm Peters, one using a nightstick and another using a metal pole. Policeman Norman Bell arrived and disarmed the drivers, then told Peters to drop his cane. Instead, "Peters jabbed the cane into the officer's stomach. Bell took a step back, and again told Peters to drop the cane. Peters swung at Bell's head. Bell blocked the blow, but Peters kicked him in the stomach. Peters turned and raised his leg *as if to deliver a karate-like side kick* (author's emphasis). Bell drew his gun and fired. The bullet entered Peter's back just below the shoulder blade. As a result, Peters was paralyzed from the chest down."

The appellate court decided in favor of Peter's estate. The District of Columbia operated under regulations providing:

...(Police officers) shall in all cases use only the minimum amount of force which is consistent with the accomplishment of his mission, and shall

exhaust every other reasonable means of apprehension or defense before resorting to the use of firearms.

The facts of this case are interesting. Peters jabbed the police officer in the stomach with his cane and there was no deadly response. Peters even kicked him in the stomach and, again, there was no deadly response. But when Peters "turned and raised his leg, as if to deliver a karate-like side kick," the cop pulled his gun and shot Peters in the back. Is it safer to jab a policeman with a cane than cock your leg for a "karate-like side kick"?

These three cases read together give a simple, but potentially life-saving, bit of advice: no matter how drunk or upset you are, don't respond to a cop by dropping into a martial arts stance. It's a good way to die with your gi on.

***

As martial artists, we are presumed to be deadly fighting machines capable of death and chaos far beyond the fighting feats of mere mortal men. If we injure someone and the matter winds up in a courtroom, our status as martial artists will likely be admissible into evidence. This elevates the nature and degree of threat beyond reality. To the jury or the judge, whose knowledge of the martial arts is shaped by Hollywood, a martial artist is not only a superior fighter, he or she is prone to fight and injure.

Also, chances are at least even that your hands and feet will be chained if your case makes it to trial, you have a history of violence and some "martial arts element" is involved.

Falling into a martial arts fighting stance when confronted by the Law is not only stupid, it is also life-threatening behavior.

CHAPTER FOUR

Martial Arts
and the
Law of
Self-Defense

Karateka Tracy Edwards was new to Milwaukee, fresh from Tupelo, Mississippi, and was no doubt anxious to meet new friends. On July 22, 1991, he asked a nice-looking, clean-cut young man to a party at his brother's house. Since his brother was not yet home, he thought nothing of it when he was invited back to his new friend's apartment to wait. With one hand cradling a beer and the other hand behind him, he admired the beautiful aquarium in his new friend's apartment. No doubt he wondered if that was the source of the nasty smell that suffused the room.

Without warning, his new acquaintance came up from behind, slapped handcuffs on the hand Edwards had behind him, and held a machete to his heart. "If you cooperate, nothing will happen to you," was all that his captor said.

Edwards remained calm, and when opportunity arose he stunned his captor with a karate blow and fled. He later led police back to the evil chambers of Jeffrey Dahmer—the cannibal who confessed to 17 dismemberment killings.

If Tracy Edwards had not launched that karate strike, he may very well have been Dahmer's 18th victim. And the monster from Milwaukee might still be killing—and eating—his victims. Who knows how many more might have died?

This may be the best example of self-defense in our generation. But self-defense is a far more complicated matter than what might be assumed. Few cases are as clear-cut as the Jeffrey Dahmer matter. Martial artists confront numerous legal issues when exercising their "right to self-defense" due to their special training.

For starters, self-defense is not a right, but a privilege—a privilege that can be lost in a variety of ways.

The following discussion of self-defense intends to set forth general legal principles, but caution is given up-front: there is no substitute for advice from a lawyer in your jurisdiction. (For example, the "duty to retreat," discussed later, is found more commonly in Northern states than Southern states.)

Self-defense issues can be raised in both civil and criminal law settings. However, subtle distinctions in this respect would complicate the analysis since self-defense, by definition, occurs in the heat of the moment. Both civil and (more often) criminal cases are cited, and as a whole the full parameters of self-defense are explored. In civil cases, the question is addressed in terms of money damages; in criminal cases, the issue is defense against incarceration—the loss of money or freedom.

The Requirement of "Apprehension"

The privilege of self-defense is triggered only where the "actor" is apprehensive about being assaulted. These fears must be reasonable. In assessing the fear, one authority suggests that the "difference in age,

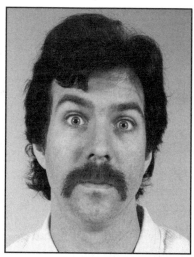

Apprehension gives rise to the privilege of self-defense. Does a martial artist's fudoshin, "calmness in a state of emergency," defeat the self-defense claim? Does a martial artist have the legal right of self-defense if he doesn't have apprehension? Should he be held to a higher standard? To a trained fighter, widening the eyes is a signal an attack is coming. As Ed Parker, kenpo grandmaster, remarked, "The eyes are the window to the soul."

size and relative strength of the parties" would be helpful. The actor must be apprehensive about serious bodily harm or death to justify self-defense with killing force. However, the actor need not fear for his life or safety to justify a *lesser* degree of force in self-defense.

It is clear that a defendant's failure to actually fear his opponent will not affect the defendant's right to self-defense. Apprehension is not the same thing as fear. For example, from the *Restatement of Torts, 2d:*

Mr. A, a scrawny individual who is intoxicated, attempts to strike Mr. B, who is the heavyweight boxing champion of the world. Mr. B is not at all afraid of Mr. A, is confident he can avoid any such blow, and in fact, succeeds in doing so. Mr. A is nevertheless subject to liability to Mr. B.

Apprehension gives rise to the privilege of self-defense, since one is permitted by law to fend off an assault. One need not fear that the intended contact will be successful; one need only believe that the act may result in imminent contact unless prevented by flight or intervention.

In 1926, the North Dakota Supreme Court heard *Powell v. Meiers.* There, the defendant and another called on the plaintiff's home to borrow a gun. Refusing the request, the plaintiff chided the defendant for taking money from her son in poker games. The defendant retorted by calling the plaintiff "ugly names" and by casting "grave imputations upon her virtue." Provoked, the plaintiff struck the defendant in the face with a kitchen towel. The defendant responded by hitting her in the eye (leaving a bruise that was visible for some two months), and by kicking her, causing some lameness. The North Dakota Supreme Court affirmed the plaintiff's recovery of $1,000 compensatory and $500 exemplary damages. The court rejected the defendant's predictable claim of self-defense, stating "a hand towel can scarcely be considered a dangerous weapon, and there is nothing to suggest that the defendant was a man of such timidity that the flourishing of a towel by a lady should fill him with alarm."

A more recent case, *State v. Brown,* is instructive. Here, defendant Glen Brown argued with Ronald Perkins during a card game. The next day, Brown ran into Perkins again, they argued, and Brown stabbed and killed Perkins with a knife. In his defense, Brown claimed "self-defense."

The statements Brown told police, that "he was not afraid of Perkins" and "he (Brown) knew karate," were used to defeat his "self-defense" claim. There was no "reasonable belief he was in imminent danger of death or serious physical injury" from his stabbing victim. Here, the "martial artist" was hoisted by his own petard. You cannot use deadly force unless you fear the same—and Brown helped convict himself by his own boasts.

In the next cases, the defendants all shot or stabbed (and in the main, killed) martial artists and then claimed "self-defense." First is the case of *People v. Mosely.* Here Brenda Mosley, the defendant, lived with her boyfriend, a correctional officer "trained in the martial arts." While breaking up, they scuffled like lovers sometimes do when the relationship terminates. She testified that he hit her, a claim he denied. She then shot a round from a .38 into the floor, then a second into her boyfriend's stomach from a distance of 10 feet. In denying her "self-defense" claim on appeal and affirming the conviction of aggravated assault, the court held it was an "unreasonable" belief that shooting the victim was "necessary to prevent her own death or great bodily harm." The court referred to another case which held "a belief that the victim, unarmed, might kill or greatly injure the defendant while she had a loaded gun, was unreasonable." The victim's status as a martial artist did not justify a shot to the gut.

In the case of *Gold v. State,* the martial artist was murdered. Mr. Gold caught Ron Kopp, a martial artist and an "old friend," in a motel with *Mrs.* Gold and they weren't watching television. A heated argument between Mr. Gold and his martial arts expert "friend" ensued. Gold, followed by Kopp, went to his car, retrieved a two-shot derringer, and ordered Kopp to back off. He did so and invited Mr. Gold back to the motel room to "discuss the situation." Upon their return, Gold shot him twice. Rejecting Gold's claim of self-defense, the court reasoned:

Kopp had a reputation as a martial arts...expert and appeared angry and threatening (when they went to the car). But by the time he returned to the room the self-defense motivation had dissipated. Kopp was no longer threatening and was in fact seated away from (Gold) when he was shot.

There was no "*reasonable* fear or apprehension." The claim of self-defense failed.

Next is the curious case of *Green v. State.* On the day he was killed by his wife, Mr. Green was visiting with another woman with whom he fathered a child. Mrs. Green, an unhappy woman, pulled up in her car, pointed a gun at one of the residents of the house, and demanded that her husband come out. A fatal mistake: he did. An argument ensued wherein Mrs. Green said her husband threatened her life. She testified that her "husband was trained in karate and that she was in fear of her life or great bodily harm." Her car would not start so she got out to walk, during which she hurled gratuitously over her shoulder that he "was not the father of *their* son," and he began to pursue her down the street. Evidence conflicts as to whether he "grabbed her or attempted to grab her but failed." She shot and killed him, and for this was convicted of voluntary manslaughter.

On appeal she claimed that she should have been found guilty of murder—or nothing at all—due to her claim of self-defense. The appellate court disagreed and found that she "acted in the heat of passion arising from (his) serious provocation," thus involuntary manslaughter—which the jury also concluded. Frankly, this was a bad call. But Georgia courts will never be quick to condone husband killing—whatever the facts. The appellate court upheld the jury verdict, and the doctrine of self-defense was dealt a deadly blow. If Mrs. Green could have proven her "reasonable fear for life," she should have walked. A bad case.

Next comes a Law of the Wierd case, *People v. Carpi.* At the time of the murder, the defendant was a 71-year-old man living in an apartment complex. He complained to the apartment management that people were "exploding firecrackers outside his window." The apartment management told him there was nothing they could do, because the persons responsible were "karate students and they were tough."

On May 6, 1975, after Mr. Carpi heard two "bangs," one after another, against his window, he looked out to see two men throwing a frisbee back and forth. Since he *believed* that at least one of them was a karate student, the septuagenarian stuck his 35-year-old gun into his waistband and headed outside.

Carpi approached Donald Wysocki and asked that he not throw things against his window. An argument ensued, after which Wysocki turned and walked away. Carpi then leaned forward and struck Wysocki on the head with the gun, which discharged and killed him. At trial, Carpi claimed—guess what—self-defense. Upholding his conviction of murder, the Illinois court opined:

On the basis of the evidence it is apparent that (Carpi) had only a general suspicion, and no specific knowledge, that Wysocki was a karate student, so that the defendant's belief, if any, that he was about to receive great bodily harm from a person trained in karate was not reasonable...under the facts of this case.

This implies somewhat that had Carpi *known* Wysocki was a karate student *(student!)*, the result might have been different. Martial artists beware. This is only a foretaste of what comes later.

Lastly is the case of *Carter v. Commonwealth*. Here, the court denied Carter's "vicarious self-defense." Carter claimed self-defense in the shooting death of Larry Alston by Larry Ellis. Ellis testified that Alston got mad when he refused to sell him marijuana and "assumed an aggressive stance, aiming kicks at him like doing karate or judo...and advanced toward him, aiming more kicks at him." Fearing injury, Ellis claimed, he pulled a gun and shot and killed Alston. (In reality, Alston was shot in the back.) Carter admitted to going through Alston's pockets (along with three other gang members, it turned out). The court held:

The foregoing versions contained no facts which would warrant the giving of a self-defense instruction in Carter's case. Arguably, they might give some support to a self-defense instruction in Ellis' favor, but Ellis was not on trial.

Therefore, the trial court did not err in refusing to give a self-defense instruction to the jury in the *Carter* trial, since Carter had no reason to fear danger to himself—even under his obviously fictitious version of the murder.

Martial artists, of course, experience the same trials and tribulations as their non-trained counterparts. However, martial artists are often able to cope with confrontation and combat with greater calm and reflection than non-martial artists. Martial arts instructors teach how to control the mind and convert fear into attack energy. These skills have definite bearing on a karateka's performance. The martial arts place a premium on *fudoshin* (the ability to remain calm in an emergency).

This presents several legal questions for martial artists. First, does the fudoshin enjoyed by martial artists prevent them from claiming self-defense? Since there *can* be apprehension while calm, martial artists can assert self-defense and make it stick.

Second, given the martial artist's superior fighting ability, both offensively and defensively, can there be "reasonable" fear that a battery will succeed? There certainly may be cases where the disparity in the plaintiff's ability to attack and the defendant martial artist's ability to defend may be as great or greater than the disparity the North Dakota Court faced in *Powell v. Meiers,* considered earlier. The preferable view, it seems, would justify self-defense sufficient to prevent the attack. But reasonable apprehension nevertheless exists in the eyes of the law. A close analogy can be drawn to this example (Mr. A. and Mr. B.), in that the puny drunk was found liable for assaulting the heavyweight boxing champion, even though the champ was in no actual danger of injury.

Third, remember in *State v. Brown,* also considered earlier, that the defendant helped defeat his own self-defense claim by saying he was "unafraid" and he "knew karate."

The Duty to Warn

The person about to defend himself may have a duty to warn the assailant of such an intention. Apparently this is true only when there is reason to believe a warning will deter the attack and allow the per-

Does a black belt martial artist have a legal duty to warn others of his fighting prowess on the theory that his martial arts skill is a "concealed deadly weapon"?

son time to defend himself, if necessary. This issue is related to "apprehension" in that it pertains to the defendant's state of mind at the time of the self-defense action.

What are the duties of martial artists to warn would-be attackers of their unique ability to frustrate such attacks? Muggings and bar-room brawls are often averted by martial artists who warn of their powers. On the other hand, martial artists nervously chuckle when hearing the old joke about the karateka who, when approached by a robber, dropped to a low stance and barked out the warning "karate!" The robber retorted "crowbar!" and proceeded to separate the martial artist from his gold. The point is clear: a warning may precipitate a more ruthless assault rather than avoid one altogether. It's a judgment call, case by case.

The case of *State v. Lane* is somewhat instructive. According to the victim Charles Clark, a martial artist, while he and the defendant Larry Lane went looking for a bar, Lane tried to rob him at gunpoint.

Lane shot the martial artist twice, but was wrestled to the ground, disarmed, then hit on the head with his own gun! As usually happens, the defendant's version of the facts differed. A pimp, Lane claimed he and the martial artist argued about the price of one of his prostitutes. He claimed the martial artist said "I'm a karate expert and I'm going to beat your ass." A scuffle ensued, during which he shot the would-be John twice before being wrestled to the ground and disarmed. Here there was certainly a clear "warning," should the pimp's testimony be believed.

The courts of this land "extend" the law every day, and stretch it to fit new circumstances. "Concealed deadly weapon" statutes are not sacrosanct. While this may not be popular among martial artists, it is my belief that one day courts will extend "concealed deadly weapon" laws to equate "concealment" with "nondisclosure" of the fighting prowess of a true martial arts expert.

You can almost hear some disingenuous local prosecutor, always looking for a headline, seducing the grand jury to indict a martial artist for aggravated assault. The charge? "Carrying a concealed deadly weapon" (his unique fighting skill). At the well-attended press conference, the prosecutor might justify this in the name of "cracking down on those martial arts *ninja* who stalk about the community as 'person-ifications of deadly weapons.'" He might reason: "Anybody with a black belt is just like a deadly weapon *concealing* their fighting ability when they could have disclosed it. This is tantamount to whipping out a secreted Saturday night special and blowing somebody away. We're not going to let these highly trained fighters skirt our concealed deadly weapons statutes; if they're going to fight, they're going to disclose their status as trained fighters first!"

Far out? Sure. Far-fetched? Maybe not. Let's look at the philosophy or "jurisprudence" of the concealed deadly weapons laws. *Why* is it legal to have a deadly weapon (in some jurisdictions) *just so long as it's not concealed?*

It goes to the issues of "fair play" and "reasonable expectations." If a man sat at a bar with a gun strapped on his hip and a bowie knife jutting out of his belt in plain view, there might not be a fight. Aware that the man with the gun and the knife could inflict punishing injury (like a martial artist), potential assailants would be *warned away.* Common sense prevails.

Martial arts experts carry numerous deadly weapons with them everywhere they go. To inventory: hands (iron palms, knuckles, fingertips, sides), feet (ball, heel, side, instep), knees, elbows, head (forehead and back) and even hips and shoulders (judo technique leverage points). These are the natural weapons that martial artists train with to become proficient fighters. What martial artist has not been asked "Do you have to register your hands and feet as deadly weapons?" (Answer: Not yet.)

There are exceptions to every rule, and each incident must be viewed in light of its own peculiar and unique circumstances. Someday, a trained fighter's duty to disclose his status as such might be the legal equivalent of advising a bully to take a better look at that boot knife dangling only inches away.

A personal example comes to mind. In 1985 I bought a home in a tough part of Louisville, Kentucky. Out jogging, I soon found myself stopped and encircled by a group of teenagers who were itching to fight. Before the first punch was thrown, I asked, "Hey, you guys ever hear of Henry Cook?" Several spoke up at once, "Yeah, man, Henry Cook is a *bad* dude, black belt fighter man." "Well," I responded, "I taught him judo 25 years ago." My would-be assailants melted away like a mint julep at the Kentucky Derby. To paraphrase Sun Tzu, the truest victory comes when there is no battle at all.

Naturally, common sense dictates sensible behavior, and usually the law is not far behind. There are times when it's wiser to take a chance with twelve jurors than to be carried by six pallbearers. There are circumstances under which disclosure of fighting prowess would only *aggravate* the situation and egg the attacker on. That's the argument for nondisclosure.

But as a matter of prophylactic legal protection, to be safe expert martial artists should disclose their fighting skill. Doing so may not only avoid jail, but may also avoid the fracas itself. Besides, disclosure of fighting skills does not *necessarily* mean the martial artist would therefore *lose* the impending brawl, right?

The Duty to Retreat

Whether one has a duty to retreat and attempt to avoid conflict prior to defending oneself depends on the degree or type of force utilized to repel the attack. In ordinary assault and battery cases, the defendant is not obligated to retreat. He or she may stand his or her ground and "use force short of that likely to cause serious physical injury." This is allowed by law even if you know with absolute certainty that you could avoid threatened bodily harm by retreating.

The issue is not as well settled where you might refuse to retreat and use *deadly* force to defend against *deadly* force. Courts are split on whether a defendant must "retreat to the wall" before using deadly force. The majority of courts, centered largely in the South and West, hold dignity and sense of honor in esteem and permit citizens to stand their ground and use deadly force against attacks that call for it. The defendant may even be privileged to *kill* his assailant. To use deadly force in self-defense, of course, you must believe that you are in danger of losing your life or are risking serious injury.

While there is *no* duty to retreat when *non-deadly force* is used by one claiming the self-defense privilege, a duty to retreat may exist where one uses or intends to use deadly force in self-defense.

There are two exceptions. First, courts have continued the ancient rule that there is no obligation to retreat when the assault takes place on the defendant's own premises. Second, the obligation to retreat is voided when the intended victim can no longer retreat safely. If there is any *reasonable* doubt, you need not run. Clearly, no court would demand "detached reflection" in the presence of a drawn gun or an upraised knife. Some suggest that the proliferation of firearms reduces "safe retreat" to a moot question since you can't out-run a bullet.

Persons trained in the martial arts should avoid street encounters as much as taxes. Martial artists should be instructed to retreat, if possible, and to stay and fight only if necessary for his own or others' safety. Martial artists should be taught to "run with confidence" from confrontations. In many encounter situations, the best self-defense, even for martial artists, is to simply run away.

The problem arises if a martial artist refuses to retreat when confronted with either deadly or non-deadly force. The assumption is that martial artists are capable of employing their hands and feet to inflict death or great bodily injury. However, martial artists are also capable of defending themselves through non-skilled methods (for example, grabbing the assailant and holding on until the danger passes). Also, martial artists can moderate the force of a kick or punch, vary a technique, or strike non-lethal areas on their assailant's body. And, of course, martial artists—like anyone else—can inflict deadly force by non-martial arts methods. Therefore, martial artists do not necessarily have to use their deadly skills in self-defense.

Four appellate court opinions discuss the martial artists' "duty to retreat." The defendant in *Commonwealth v. Glass* was a knife fighter trained by the United States Marine Corps. Defendant Glass explained he was taught at boot camp to make a turning, double-thrust motion with the knife "because the turning motion creates more injury." Glass had been at a party comprised mainly of Vietnamese. For reasons unclear, an argument took place after Glass was pushed from the front steps. Though in the eyes of the court "he could clearly have fled," he pulled a knife and stabbed four Vietnamese, one fatally, and chased two of them to their own homes to stab them. Clearly, these were not the actions of one acting in "self-defense."

An equally strange case is *People v. Flax.* Barry Flax, a *jujitsu* black belt, went into Zip's Place, a bar, and attempted to check his "Japanese (expanding) baton" in with the owner, who slapped it out of his hands and told him to get out of the bar. Flax left the bar, went home, and retrieved his 12-gauge shotgun. He returned to the bar and quite a gunfight ensued, and as a result several fell to Flax's unfriendly fire. The court held that when Flax went home for his gun he had "retreated from the fight and reached a place of safety." Flax's justification to use deadly force "vanishes when the defendant is able to make his escape."

Next is the case of *Commonwealth v. Palmer.* Clifton Palmer and Eugene Ross got into an argument over women (imagine that!) and Palmer was forced to leave the house they shared with several other people. He obtained a shotgun and returned, with the gun hid in a guitar case. Palmer knew Ross was trained in karate, so he "was both respectful and fearful of Ross' physical prowess." After seeing Palmer at the house again, Ross pursued him across the street and around his car. Palmer whipped the shotgun out and told the martial artist to back off. Instead, Ross charged and was shot in the hand, and an innocent child was killed. In reversing the guilty verdicts, the court held that "if Palmer believed he was 'cornered' or without an avenue of retreat...he was justified in using deadly force."

Under the Pennsylvania statutes, self-defense under these circumstances was allowed unless "the defendant knows he can avoid the necessity of using such force with complete safety by retreating." This is an interesting side note: the court assumed the unarmed martial artist was as deadly as the shotgun! Otherwise, the defendant's use of deadly force would have been disallowed altogether.

Lastly is the case of *Commonwealth v. Lapointe.* Defendant Daniel Lapointe got into an argument over the telephone with Edward LeBlanc, the ex-husband of Lapointe's current live-in girlfriend. LeBlanc, a black belt martial artist, went to Lapointe's house. When Lapointe unlocked the dead bolt, "an enraged LeBlanc rushed in, his arms in the air," and advanced on the defendant. Lapointe pumped six bullets from his Walther .380 automatic gun into the martial artist, and killed him instantly.

The court held that "the right to use deadly force by way of self-defense is not available to one threatened until he has availed himself of all reasonable and proper means in the circumstances to avoid combat." This rule has equal protection to one assaulted or threatened in his home by a "lawful visitor." Though unwelcome, the dead martial artist *was* a "lawful visitor." Perhaps the self-defense claim would have worked had Lapointe retreated down the hall before firing. Further, the court upheld the doctrine that "excessive force in self-defense warrants a conviction of manslaughter." Unlike the previous case, *Commonwealth v. Palmer,* the instant court did not accord the victim's black belt status in and of itself as "deadly force," thus permitting deadly self-defense.

The Question of "Excessive Force"

To avoid liability for the use of excessive force in self-defense, you may use only such force in repelling the attack as a "reasonable" person would have thought necessary under the circumstances. This is characterized as "reasonable force." No greater force than is necessary to protect yourself is permissible. In other words, the force used in self-defense must be proportionate to the harm which you seek to avoid. For example, you are not privileged to use deadly force to prevent the infliction of a slight harm. A good illustration of this "proportionate force" doctrine is found in *Bannister v. Mitchell,* a case decided by the Virginia Supreme Court. The defendant was brawling with the plaintiff's brother, a small one-legged man, when the plaintiff intervened by striking the defendant with her umbrella. The defendant's "self-defense" was to cut the female assailant with a pocketknife from cheek to ear. Affirming for the woman a judgment of $650 in damages, the Virginia Supreme Court held that the force employed by the defendant was not proportionate. Moreover, "the use of his knife...under the circumstances was entirely unnecessary for his own protection."

There is one qualification: If you realize that someone attacking you with deadly force is incapable of achieving his purpose, you are not privileged to use deadly force in self-defense. I was once attacked by a small woman with a knife. I disarmed her easily without harming her. Given my background in the martial arts, I was *not* entitled

Is the disparity in size between the attacker and the defender mitigated when a knife is pulled?

to kill her and claim "self-defense." The common law is based on common sense.

In determining whether the force used in self-defense is reasonable or excessive, American courts have looked at a number of factors. Some courts look to the amount of force exerted, the means employed to exert the force, the manner in which the force was applied, and the surrounding circumstances. Other courts have also looked to the parties themselves, considering such things as the relative age, size and strength of the parties, their reputations for violence, and the identity of the aggressor.

Here are four examples of how a court might view the following incidents:

1. A man attempts to strike you with his fists. You are not privileged to knock him down if you can easily prevent him from striking you by holding his arms.

2. A man attempts to prevent you from leaving a room by standing in the only doorway. You are much larger than the other man and can readily push him out of the way. You are not privileged to knock him down.

3. A weak old man attempts to attack you with a knife. It is obvious to you that you can disarm the old man with perfect safety. You are not privileged to shoot him with a gun.

4. A man attempts to attack you. You size up the situation and can easily avoid his attack and disarm him. You are not privileged to confine that man in a room where you keep a ferocious watchdog. *(Restatement of Torts, 2d.)*

One using excessive force to repel an attack not only loses the right to assert self-defense, but also may become liable to the original aggressor for damages. In 1870 the Indiana Supreme Court decided *Adams v. Waggoner*. The plaintiff and defendant fought by mutual consent. The defendant became angry and stabbed the plaintiff three times. In affirming a verdict awarding the plaintiff damages, the Indiana Supreme Court held:

It is a settled doctrine of the law, that if one be attacked he may defend himself using no more force than may be necessary to repel the attack; but should he go beyond this, and use more than necessary, he becomes a trespasser himself, and his assailant, though first in the wrong, may maintain against him an action for damages.

It is generally understood that the defendant may be privileged to use much greater force in self-defense when the attack is by multiple assailants than when it is by a single assailant. The defendant becomes privileged by law to use force against a number of attackers that would be deemed excessive against one attacker. The justification for allowing defense by more forcible means when there are several assailants is that "a person assaulted by a mob...is necessarily...subject to greater terror and apprehension than when the assault is made by an individual..." *(Higgins v. Minaghan)*

Three more recent cases (this century) pit martial artists against guns. In each instance, the court found the gun-wielder exceeded, and thus lost, the force necessary for self-defense. In *Johnson v. State,* the defendant admitted that he murdered the martial artist with a gun, "but claimed it was done in self-defense because of his fear that the victim might use some karate moves on him, take his gun away, and kill him." The court was unimpressed and noted "(t)hree eyewitnesses testified at trial to the shooting and stated that the victim was unarmed and made no moves or threatening gestures..." Similarly, another martial artist was shot to death in *Harris v. State,* here by an irate girlfriend.

She testified that she "was threatened by Hackner and picked up a gun which was lying on a table in order to keep (him) away from her; when he continued to come after her, she shot him." Hackner was a cop and "was skilled in the martial arts." The defendant argued "that because of the vast difference in size between Hackner and herself, as well as Hackner's specialized training, the use of a gun in defending against his attack did not constitute unreasonable force." Neither the jury nor the appellate court bought the argument, and they upheld the second-degree murder conviction. The court took into account that "witnesses attested to the defendant's propensities for violence as well as Hackner's demonstrated restraint when he was previously attacked by the defendant." The case of *Harris v. Pineset* grew out of an argument at a bar. Pineset testified "plaintiff (Harris) proceeded to Pineset's table, kicking a chair on the way and threatening to 'chop-up' Pineset using karate if he refused to follow (him) outside. Once outside, a scuffle ensued and Pineset shot the martial artist in the abdomen." The court held that use of the pistol amounted to "excessive force under the circumstances." The court reasoned:

Pineset's use of the pistol is not justifiable because, under these circumstances, Pineset's fear of a fight with plaintiff, who was physically smaller than Pineset, would not be likely to produce similar emotions in men of reasonable prudence. A reasonable man would not have found it necessary to use a gun to repel the plaintiff in any physical encounter that might have occurred.

The martial artist won damages approaching $200,000 "with legal interest thereon until paid."

When you get down to it, what do martial artists do? They practice fighting. It is the very nature of the beast that their capacity for *skilled* unarmed combat approaches perfection. Trained fighters can be expected to possess a high degree of judgment when confronted with fighting situations. With this training, and given a proper attitude, a martial artist should be able to extricate himself from many situations without ever having to use excessive force.

Martial artists are trained to conform their self-defense to the seriousness of the attack. Gnats are not blasted with cannons. Neither are offensive, but reasonably harmless, drunks dealt with by deadly force. As one martial art instructor stated:

You have to teach retaliation situations. If a person's just a drunk, you deal with him one way. If it's a group of hoodlums, you deal with them another way. And if it's a guy coming at you with a broken beer bottle, you deal with that another way.

An example of measured and appropriate response to attack can be found in *Dun's Review:*

At 46, Jerome Gillman, vice president of Richard Weiner Associates, a New York-based public relations firm, is not a violent man. But when 'three big apes' jumped Gillman on a deserted Manhattan street late one night and demanded his wallet, the mild-mannered, 184-pound Gillman 'instinctively did my homework...' He applied an elbow lock to the leader of the pack, neatly executed a classic nage waza and sent the startled mugger crashing to the sidewalk, rendering him 'slightly unconscious.' The other two punks fled in panic. They had made the mistake of accosting a business executive who happens to hold a second-degree black belt in judo.

Several unique questions are posed for martial artists by the issue of *reasonable* versus *excessive* force. First, it is feared than an unspoken presumption may subject "deadly fighters" to liability for "excessive force" used in self-defense (due more to the characterization of the actor than the analysis of the particular facts and circumstances). What juries and legislators must be shown is that a mere *capacity* for deadly force does not mean that the ability will ever be used. For martial artists, this presents a problem of proof and a problem of keeping inflammatory and legally irrelevant proof from the jury. The earlier cases of *Harris v. Pineset, Harris v. State* and *Johnson v. State* indicate judges and juries tend not to automatically label martial artists as aggressors.

Martial artists have a wide-ranging arsenal at their disposal, from which they can spontaneously custom-make an appropriate defense. Not all self-defense should be presumed "excessive force," merely because it emanates from one with the ability to inflict excessive force. Instead of using deadly force, the martial artist can, for example:

—"Pull" his or her punches or kicks, as is done at non-contact karate tournaments to minimize injury.

—Strike or kick areas of the assailant's body which are not particularly sensitive or vulnerable, e.g., the side of the arm or right side of the chest as opposed to the groin or throat.

In a confrontation, you can avoid using deadly force by striking non-vital areas and pulling the kick or punch.

—Throw the attacker on his back gently instead of on his head forcefully.

—Armlock, wristlock or pin the attacker with judo or jujitsu techniques.

If courts and legislatures accept the fact that martial artists can be selective in devising a defense, a different problem may be raised for the trained fighter. When one has been injured by a martial artist claiming self-defense, courts may look to the seriousness of the injury, and assume that since the martial artist can select his or her defense, the nature of the injuries dictates whether the martial artist opted to use excessive force. Such a legal position would be unfortunate. While martial arts experts can ready-make a defense, they cannot control all combat circumstances. Assailants have been known to run face-first into the unexpected foot of a karateka. And while the *aikido* master may merely intend to subdue the attacker by armlock until help arrives, he cannot prevent the aggressor from squirming—thus breaking his own arm.

Courts could well inquire as to:

—What technique, if any, did the martial artist undertake to use and with what force?

—The physical characteristics of the martial artist compared with those of the other party.

The second issue here deals with intent. In some cases it will not be relevant whether the martial artist *intended* to use excessive force. In others, it could become crucial. The danger is that courts may attribute this "intent to use excessive force" to martial artists due to their special

The judo throw *deashi barai* begins from (1) the normal holding position. (2-4) As your attacker steps forward toward you,

training. This is logically indefensible. Much occurs in street combat beyond the control of even a well-trained and skilled fighter. Where this question of "intent to use excessive force" becomes an issue, courts should require the plaintiff to only bear his burden of proof, and indulge no "deadly fighter" presumption in knee-jerk fashion.

Under the right set of facts, a court could consider a range of possible defenses open to a martial artist. The implicit assumption is that expert martial artists are trained fighters. We conscientiously train in various defenses to counter the myriad of possible attacks. For example, if an expert karateka were attacked, he or she could simply block punches and kicks until the assailant gave up the attack. If an expert jujitsu practitioner were attacked, he or she could lock a limb, without breaking it, until the assailant submitted or the authorities arrived. If an expert *judoka* were attacked, he or she could apply *shime-waza* (strangulation techniques) to the assailant until the assailant surrendered or painlessly lost consciousness. If an expert aikido student were attacked, he or she could repeatedly throw the assailant on his back until the assailant wearied. On the other hand, the karateka could block, then strike a killing blow to the temple; the jujitsu expert could break each and every one of the assailant's four limbs; the judoka could

lift your left foot and sweep his right foot at his ankle while turning to the left. Your attacker loses his balance and falls easily.

continue the strangulation after the assailant lost consciousness until he died; or the aikido expert could throw the assailant face-first onto the sidewalk.

If the martial artist has a true choice between both alternatives, only the former, less forceful, defense may remain privileged.

Third, there is reason to treat martial artists *differently* than non-martial artists when they are assaulted by multiple assailants. The law permits a non-trained fighter to use greater force in self-defense against gangs than against single attackers, the justification being that the overpowering odds and greatly increased apprehension warrants the actor to use greater force in self-defense. Martial artists, however,

A *jujitsu* armlock such as the one shown here can defuse your attacker in short work.

should not automatically be granted privilege to use *excessive* force against multiple assailants. For the expert martial artist, the odds are not overwhelming and the apprehension is not greatly increased. In fact, martial artists are taught to use the presence of multiple assailants to good advantage by "playing them off against one another" and defeating them one by one. For example, if attacked by three assailants, the trained fighter would typically hurl one into another and quickly turn his attention to finish off the third. Of the remaining two, the martial artist would maneuver one in front of the other, incapacitate the assailant in front, then devote attention to the third and final assailant, who is likely by this point to be on the run!

This, of course, works better in theory than in practice. Nevertheless, it often works as described. Courts should look to the manner of defense and progression of the combat to see if the martial artist is entitled to exoneration by virtue of self-defense.

In any event, no *automatic* privilege to use deadly force should be granted when the "victim" of a gang attack is an expert martial artist. If the "playing off" strategy succeeds, the martial artist should be no freer to use a deadly blow on a gang member than on a single assailant.

Fourth, the "reasonable force" standard itself must be re-evaluated when dealing with martial artists. Reasonable force is that force which a reasonable, prudent man thinks necessary under the circumstances.

When an expert martial artist is accused of excessive force in self-defense, the standard should be higher, that of a "reasonable, prudent, expert *martial artist.*" It is only fair that one with unique skills is held to a unique standard.

The force a person may use in self-defense is that which seems necessary to fend off an attack and prevent injury. Easily stated, this sounds simple. In reality, this tit-for-tat force can be precisely gauged or measured by only a seasoned fighter—in and out of the *dojo.*

Hindsight, of course, remains 20/20. Hence, courts consider the circumstances at the time of the altercation. The defendant using self-defense is "not required to (have) nicely measure(d) or narrowly gauge(d) the force to the amount required from a deliberate retrospective view." *(Conklin v. Borfield)* Accordingly, at least if the defendant is facing a dangerous attack, he or she will not be held liable in damages for failing "to anticipate the precise effect of a blow with the fist." *(Dupre v. Maryland Management Co.)*

Courts will take into account the "heat of conflict" and the "impending peril" the defendant faces when repelling an attack.

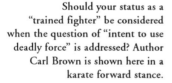

Should your status as a "trained fighter" be considered when the question of "intent to use deadly force" is addressed? Author Carl Brown is shown here in a karate forward stance.

Typically, unless the force used in self-defense was "so excessive as clearly to be vindictive under the circumstances," the defendant will not be judged to have exceeded his privilege. *(6 AM JUR 162)*

(a) Passive defenses are available to the *karateka*—block after block, here is a top block, common in most styles.

(b) Or, the karateka can strike. This could mean he'll strike out in court, unless the case for self-defense is clear.

(c) To play it safe, at least safer in terms of legal consequences, the judoka defends himself with an armlock.

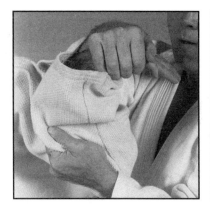 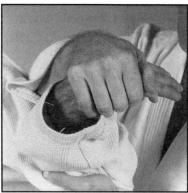

In the *jujitsu* practitioner's arsenal are wrist and elbow locks custom-made for "low level" reaction to attack. (An incorrect application of force can result in a broken elbow, broken wrist, or both.)

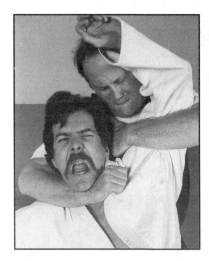 

Properly applied, the *judoka's kata juji jime* of the *shime waze,* strangulation techniques, can knock out the opponent within seconds since it can constrict the flow of blood to the brain.

If the *judoka* chooses *hadaka jime* instead, oxygen can be cut off. Brain damage can occur.

(Use caution.)

Martial artists are masters of measuring force. Karateka cleave melons placed on the bare stomachs of assistants by slicing samurai swords down to within a fraction of an inch of their assistants' skin. Jujitsu

Carl Brown and his assistant Richard Loeb demonstrate an *aikido* throw. When Brown (right) is attacked with an overhead left hammerfist, he (1) catches Loeb's momentum and (2) redirects it

experts apply only so much pressure to the limbs of their practice partners as necessary to execute the technique without breaking bones. Judoka know with some intuitive precision the force needed to strangle a competitor into unconsciousness—not death. Aikido masters can throw opponents at varying velocities.

The simple explanation for this ability to measure force is the intense and constant practice of these techniques by martial artists. Measurement of force becomes second nature to skilled fighters. Since it is essential for their practice partner to avoid serious injury, martial artists must be able to "pull" their punches and kicks, "ease" their armlocks and chokes, and "soften" their partner's impact when

Confronted with the identical attack as above, Brown could just as easily use his left hand to (1-2) slam the attacker's face into the pavement, thereby inflicting deadly force.

in a downward circular movement. Wishing to injure his attacker as little as possible, Brown (2-4) blocks the attacker's head with his left hand, allowing him to complete the fall.

thrown to the mat. Martial artists can testify as "expert witnesses" regarding the "reasonableness" of the self-defense used by martial artist defendants.

Not many years ago, a karate instructor was acquitted of the self-defense slaying of his father. The issue of excessive force was raised. The assailant's father, also a karate instructor, attacked his son with a sword following an argument over taxes. The defendant fought a pitched battle with his father for 20 to 25 minutes, then tied *nunchaku* (wooden sticks held together with nylon chain or rope) around his father's throat, intending to cut off his air supply and subdue him. Instead, he inadvertently used too much force and killed him. The martial artist's ability to measure force was the dominant issue at trial.

The fifth and final self-defense factor is the physical disparity, if any, between the attacker and the defender. This entails more than a simple comparison of height, weight, age and body build. Attention is paid to the relative ability of each party to harm the other. "An invalid with a loaded automatic in his hand can be more dangerous and cause much more terror than an unarmed, heavily muscled wrestler."

Several courts have held that "disparity of parties" is conducive to findings of "excessive force," impairing the self-defense privilege. Five such cases add some flavor to the facts where physically superior defendants made self-defense pleas. In *Lyon v. Commonwealth*,

The "reasonable force" standard may be modified against you if you've had martial arts training.

the court rejected the defendant's self-defense plea when the defendant beat and kicked his 65-years-or-older, 135-pound father-in-law for insulting him and shaking a fist in his face. Affirming the "large verdict" of a $500 fine and ten months imprisonment, the Kentucky Court of Appeals stressed that "it must be remembered that this was an aggravated case. Appellant Lyon was a young, able-bodied man while his father-in-law was an old, frail man who was nothing in the hands of Lyon." The following year, the Oklahoma Criminal Court of Appeals heard *Gober v. State*. In affirming the defendant's conviction for "assault and battery with force likely to cause death," the court held that the severe kicking and bruising inflicted upon the victim was unnecessary since the defendant outweighed him by some 100 pounds "and, no doubt, would have easily handled him, were it necessary, without resort to extreme violence." The Tennessee Supreme Court addressed this same issue in *Etter v. State*. The victim had lost all his money to the defendant in a craps game. Angered, the victim threw a rock (it missed) at the defendant, then proceeded to strike the defendant with his fists. Allegedly in self-defense, the defendant pulled a knife and killed the sore loser. In affirming the voluntary manslaughter conviction, the Tennessee Supreme Court stated:

In sports as well as fair play, in human relations opponents are pitted against one another who ordinarily are proportionately matched. It is a well-recognized principle of law that when one is beset with a single personal assault, not made by one of overpowering strength and force, the resistance thereto must be proportionate to the nature of the assault. In this case, the (defendant) was a much heavier man than the deceased... We can see no justification for the use of a knife.

Consistent with these opinions is *State v. McLeod*. Here, the participants' proportions were reversed, and the ruling reflected it. The defendant, a 63-year-old man with hands crippled by arthritis, squirted ammonia through his screen door at a 27-year-old ex-soldier who had threatened him. Recognizing the defendant's right to self-defense, the court emphasized the "physical disparity between the parties here."

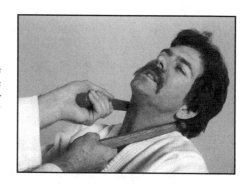

The issue of "excessive force" was raised in a case that involved "death by *nunchaku.*"

In *Jones v. Commonwealth,* the Kentucky Court of Appeals ruled similarly. The defendant's wife had consulted with an attorney about divorcing the defendant. During the consultation, the lawyer allegedly raped her. Enraged at hearing this, the defendant grabbed the attorney on the sidewalk outside his law office and severely beat and kicked him. Affirming the conviction for assault with intent to kill, the Kentucky court remarked in dicta:

Where there was great disparity in the ages of the parties or in their physical conditions, the older or weaker may be justified in using a deadly weapon to repel a violent attack by the other, although the assailant may be unarmed. But this consideration is available only for the purpose of preventing the defendant's otherwise perfect self-defense from being destroyed.

If the trained fighter uses "excessive force" in self-defense, he or she may thereby destroy the self-defense privilege and be prosecuted. This was the holding in *Lyon v. Commonwealth* (the defendant hit his old and weak father-in-law). The Kentucky Court of Appeals analyzed the legal consequences of excessive force in the following terms:

Appellant knew...(he) could easily defend himself against any assault which Scott (the son-in-law) might make on him. In other words, (he) was in no danger. In assault and battery, one may use such force only as is reasonably necessary to ward off the assault and to protect himself, but he cannot, without incurring (criminal) liability, go beyond this and inflict upon his assailant any greater injury than is necessary to stop him.

The Illinois Court of Appeals acted in accord with its 1971 *People v. Atkins* opinion. Following a minor automobile accident, the defendant and his victim stepped from their respective cars. As the victim started to reach into his pocket, the defendant knocked him to the ground and kicked him until he was unconscious. Affirming the defendant's conviction for aggravated battery, the Illinois court remarked that even if it should accept that the defendant acted in self-defense, his "conduct was far beyond that which was necessary to defend himself."

The most graphic case involving the use of a deadly weapon (in the context of disparity of parties) is *Davis v. State,* decided by the Supreme Court of Indiana. The defendant, a 54-year-old, one-armed man, quarreled with the "victim," then voluntarily left the argument hoping to avoid a physical confrontation. A short time later, the victim—unarmed, but stout and robust—rushed at the defendant, who responded by shooting a gun at him. Because the jury had been erroneously instructed on the defendant's right to self-defense, the Indiana Supreme Court reversed the defendant's conviction of assault with intent to murder. As to these erroneous instructions, the court noted:

These instructions inform the jury that a person assaulted by another, who has no weapons in his hands...is not justified in using a deadly weapon in defense of his person. If that is the law, then in every conceivable case of a violent attack upon one by another, no matter what the circumstances may be, no matter what the disparity between the ages and physical strength of the two may be, the assaulted party must stand and take his chances of being knocked down and stamped into jelly, or of being choked to death before he can lawfully use a weapon in his defense... This is not the law.

Some of these cases discuss the "measure of force" and "excessive force" as though force employed to repel an attack could be gauged with precision. Courts facing the question, however, indicate that the defendant will not be held to some impossibly strict, neat measure, but will be allowed latitude given the "impending peril." As the Missouri Supreme Court stated in *State v. Hopkins:* "It is well settled that a person is not required to nicely gauge the amount of force necessary to repel an attack, but that he may act on appearances." The law will not require some "nice distinction as to the least amount of force necessary." "Measure of force" is a matter for properly instructed juries to decide on a case-by-case basis.

Anticipatory Attack

Because of extensive and rigorous practice, martial artists can be expected to possess a high degree of judgment when it comes to fight situations. If this training is coupled with a proper attitude, martial artists should be able to extricate themselves from many situations without ever having to use excessive force. Martial artists are instructed to adapt to the nature of the attack—that is, to vary self-defense postures and techniques to suit the danger encountered.

If the defendant reasonably knows that he or she is about to be attacked, he may resort to self-defense *before* being actually struck. The defendant "need not wait until the assault is made." As stated by the North Carolina Court of Appeals in *State v. Evans:* "The right to act in self-defense may arise from apparent danger." According to the Missouri Supreme Court's language in *State v. Daugherty,* the "right of attack, in some circumstances, may be essential to the right of self-defense." The *Daugherty* court discussed "anticipatory attack" thusly:

A person about to be attacked is not bound to wait until his adversary gets 'the drop on him' or 'draws bead on him,' to use familiar, but sig-

nificant expressions, before he takes steps to prevent these occurrences from taking place.

A reasonable prerequisite for this right of "anticipatory attack" seems to be that the defendant be "without fault himself." It is equally clear that not all circumstances will allow martial artists to strike first.

One consequence of the training martial artists undergo is that they acquire a "sixth sense" about attack, or as coined in Japanese—*genshin.* This "attack radar" warns expert martial artists of sudden danger. This is best illustrated by a favorite martial arts anecdote:

A master swordsman wanted to test his three best samurai disciples. He balanced a pillow over the door so that as each of them would enter one by one, the pillow would fall on them, like a surprise attack from an enemy. The first one stabbed the pillow after it hit him and bounced to the floor. The second sliced it in mid-air. The third student—who became the master's successor—did not enter the room, since he sensed the trick before it could happen.

Genshin has its roots in training and experience. Martial artists know and watch for the body language that precedes an attack. For example, my judo *sensei* instructed never to watch the hands or feet of a prospective assailant; instead, watch the eyes. A person's eyes noticably widen an instant before an assault. The eyes telegraph the impending attack. It's been expressed as follows:

Is there really such a thing as a 'sucker punch'? I tend to think not. If I am a martial artist in the true sense of the word, I'm going to be aware that something is about to happen, and I should be able to react to it.

The right to self-defense by anticipatory attack is allowed only when the defendant reasonably believes an attack is imminent. This is an area where martial artists should be judged by what other martial artists would find reasonable. This can be justified since martial artists will not only perceive an impending attack sooner than an untrained counterpart, but will also be more accurate in the perception. Of course, this special standard might breed inconsistent verdicts. There could be circumstances where the anticipatory attack of a martial artist would be reasonable, and therefore privileged, but the anticipatory attack of a non-martial artist under identical conditions would not be privileged. However, since martial artists are better able than laypersons to sense an attack, this inconsistency of result has a reasonable basis. Martial artists should not be penalized for keen sensory perception. Doing so puts a premium on late—perhaps fatally late—reaction time.

Deadly Force Against A Trained Fighter

Several cases previously addressed presented facts wherein deadly force was used against trained fighters. By and large American courts, to their credit, have not equated martial arts training as instantly equivalent to deadly force. It seems that the "the-other-person-knew-karate-and-thus-I-was-scared-and-shot-him" defense has not fared particularly well in the courtroom.

To conclude this analysis of deadly force, a few more cases need review. First is the case of *Wilson v. State*. Martial artist Larry Johnson and his friend were sparring in a parking lot, "acting out karate," during which time Johnson bumped into the car belonging to Buel David Wilson. According to the court's opinion and recitation of facts, Wilson "got out of his car with a pistol and held it in both hands aiming it at about eye-level. He made the statement 'I'll teach you to bump into my car,' and shot the martial artist in the chest, killing him." The court rejected the self-defense claim and upheld the conviction of first-degree murder, but reversed on other grounds.

Next is the case of *State v. Horton*. An argument between two co-workers resulted in the following:

During the argument defendant walked to the trunk of his car and removed a single-barrel, 12-gauge shotgun. Defendant leveled the gun at the deceased, who was approximately 10 feet away. Deceased began backing up with his hands empty and held in the air. Defendant then cocked the hammer on the shotgun and shot deceased in the stomach. After reloading the shotgun, defendant replaced it in the trunk of his automobile and drove away from the station. Kelly Winborne died as a result of the shotgun wound to his stomach.

Horton did not deny shooting the victim, but contended that the gun just "went off," and said further that "he shot Kelly

Winborne because he thought the deceased was going to kill him with 'Kung Fu.'" This pathetic "self-defense" claim did not sway the jury or the appellate court, and the first-degree murder conviction was affirmed.

The facts of *State v. Glenn* are just as straightforward. Here, the defendant slapped a martial artist's sister during an argument over whether she would get an abortion. The martial artist went to the defendant's house and a fight ensued. Glenn pulled a knife and stabbed the martial artist several times, claiming he "feared for his safety because (the victim) had studied martial arts." The court rejected this defense and implicitly held that Glenn "exceeded his self-defense privilege and thus lost it when pulling the knife." A good decision; a *fine* one, in fact.

The next case, *State v. Nielsen,* is pithy and deserves to be reported in full: "Defendant, 37 years old, attempted to rob a filling station. The attendant advised the defendant that he knew kung fu, did a kung fu scream, and jumped into a kung fu stance. Defendant shot the attendant three times in the head." *Res ipsa loquitur!*

The best was saved for last: *Echizenya v. Armenio.* "The undisputed facts are: At the time of the incident in suit plaintiff, an instructor in karate, was 31 years of age; defendant Armenio was 71 years of age. Plaintiff and a companion, both Japanese nationals, stopped in front of defendant's restaurant at approximately 11:30 p.m. on February 15, 1975, and either both or one of them commenced to urinate openly and publicly on the sidewalk or at the restaurant's front entrance door. Both plaintiff and his companion were intoxicated. Upon viewing this act, Armenio went out of his restaurant and demanded the urinating cease and the two remove themselves from his property. The content of the conversation among the parties at this point is contradictory, but is clear plaintiff and his companion refused to cease their activities and refused to remove themselves from the premises. There is some evidence Armenio became enraged, and cursed and swore at the plaintiff and his companion. Armenio then re-entered his restaurant and returned with a handgun. His partner, Toschi, accompanied him.

"Only three eyewitnesses testified to the facts of the occurrence— the plaintiff himself, Armenio and Toschi—the latter two being defense witnesses and their testimony is conflicting and often confusing.

"Plaintiff's version of the incident was that his companion was uri- nating near the entrance of the restaurant when Armenio came out and told them to desist and move. He conceded they refused to leave when Armenio requested or told them to do so. An argument ensued during which Armenio cursed and abused the two men. Armenio then went back into the restaurant and, accompanied by Toschi, returned with the handgun. Armenio then told them to remove themselves from his property on penalty of being shot. Plaintiff responded, 'Well, go ahead and shoot me,' at which time Armenio shot him in the leg. Plaintiff denied any physical encounter but admitted he was attempt- ing to hit Toschi when he was shot and that he had 'pushed' Toschi.

"The defense version, according to the testimony of Armenio and Toschi, is basically the following: Through a glass window Armenio saw the two men urinating at the front door entrance to the restaurant. He went to the door, remonstrated with them and requested them to leave. They refused to do so, got into an argument and continued to urinate with one of them actually urinating on him, Armenio. He re-entered the restaurant, told his wife to call the police, got his handgun and went back through the door with Toschi, who had been eating in the restau- rant. When, with the handgun in evidence, Armenio again told the men to leave, they still refused to do so. Further argument ensued and Armenio and Toschi were attacked by the plaintiff and his companion. Toschi was struck in the chest and forehead. Armenio was struck first in the chest and then, by an only partially successful karate 'chop,' in the neck. Plaintiff then kicked at Armenio, the kick striking the hand in which he was holding the gun. The blow accidentally caused the gun to fire and the resulting shot struck the plaintiff in the leg."

The martial artist brought a suit against Armenio for damages and lost both at trial and on appeal. Write this one off as a lawsuit that should never have been brought. The karate instructor still probably gets kidded about this one. After all, it's not every karate instructor who can kick a pistol with such precision as to shoot himself in the leg—and then sue!

Prejudice Against the Martial Artist

The fear that every martial artist must take into a fight is more than just whether he or she will be injured. The martial artist must also fear both criminal prosecution and civil lawsuits. This is why trained fighters must study and understand these fundamentals of self-defense.

In most instances, judges and the juries they instruct have acted with an intelligence common to the common law. However, once we martial artists are criminal or civil defendants, we can never be sure. The issue that arises is whether evidence of martial arts skill would outweigh its possible prejudice. This is about stereotyping. Television is our God and it teaches us that martial artists are the quintessential warriors. Naturally, in the real world, this must be tempered by questions such as:

—The particular martial art in question (frankly, not all martial arts are equally effective);

—the length of time the martial artist has studied and/or taught;

—the physical disparities between the parties in a self-defense fracas; (As Dr. Jigaro Kano, founder of *kodokan* judo put it, "a good, *big* judoka will defeat a smaller, good judoka all things but size being equal.")

—the circumstances of the fracas;

—and the weapon being defended against (a fist? A foot in a steel-toed combat boot? A knife? Nunchaku? An uzi?).

The case of *Commonwealth v. Oram* is instructive. Jack Oram was convicted of manslaughter and assault and battery by means of a dangerous weapon. There was highly conflicting evidence concerning the events leading to the death of the victim. The jury was presented with difficult questions as to whether Oram was in any degree an aggressor and whether he acted reasonably in self-defense. The court held that "the trial judge reasonably received evidence concerning Oram's knowledge of karate, limited to the means of self-defense available to him." The judge, in his discretion, could properly conclude that the relevance of this evidence outweighed its possible prejudice.

The *Oram* decision is one of those cases that leaves an important question dangling and unanswered. Oram was convicted at trial of manslaughter and assault and battery by means of a dangerous weapon. What was the dangerous weapon? Was it some object or was it Oram's "deadly martial arts ability"? In any event, the case stands for the proposition that there is a balancing test between "the relevance of the evidence" and "possible prejudice to the jury."

Overview

To summarize:

—There must be reasonable apprehension of attack before the self-defense privilege vests.

—There may be a duty to retreat from your attacker.

—Less likely, there may be a duty to warn your assailant of your fighting skill—at least where it doesn't just "fan the flames."

—Do not use excessive force in self-defense. Hurt your attacker as little as possible unless confronted with deadly force—a gun or knife—then go all out. And in some circumstances, even then deadly force is not justified.

—Martial artists have a legitimate and unique claim to "preemptive anticipatory attack" due to special alertness to assault.

—Beware the "I shot him because he came at me with kung fu" scenario.

—While evidence of being a martial artist is almost always prejudicial, it may be allowed for sake of relevance, depending on the facts.

CHAPTER FIVE

Martial Arts Weapons and the Law: What's Legal in your State

Most styles of "empty hand" fighting teach the use of weapons. Students are usually taught how to use staffs of various lengths, ceremonial swords and other oriental weapons.

To a lesser extent, they are also taught how to use *nunchaku, shuriken (shaken)* and *manrikigusari.* These three weapons are far and away the forbidden fruit of American law. A definition of the terms, and a history of these weapons, is in order.

But first, an acknowledgement needs to be made. Of great help, and liberally relied upon, is testimony before the United States Senate Judiciary Committee, which on October 16, 1985, probed the "mailing of dangerous martial arts weapons." (Senate Bill 1363 (hereinafter S.1363)).

Of the seventeen Senators on the Committee, only two showed up and actively participated (Kennedy, D-Mass, and Simon, D-Ill). One other made an appearance and asked three questions (Grassley, R-Iowa), and another merely had staff minions submit a "prepared state-

Shuriken

ment" (Thurman, R-S.C.). Interestingly, Thurman co-sponsored this legislation, yet failed to show up for the Subcommittee Hearing! Of the 435 members of the House, none testified and only one (Representative Olympia J. Snowe) submitted a "prepared statement."

The bill seeks to prohibit the transport of certain martial arts weapons, namely the nunchaku, the shuriken and the manrikigusari, via the U.S. Postal Service. By its terms, S. 1363 excludes "knife,

Nunchaku

sword, or ceremonial or collector weapons" from its definition of dangerous martial arts weapons. So what if martial arts weapons are banned from delivery by mail? The 196 pages of the Senate Judiciary Committee Hearing answers that with a mixed chorus of voices.

And bear in mind, S. 1363 has not been defeated; it has just been "tabled." Both Miyamoto Musashi and Sun Tzu warned that warriors are most vulnerable just after a (perceived) victory. So read this chapter with care. You may be called upon one day to write letters to the editor, and to your congressman or congresswoman.

Before launching headlong into an analysis of the legislation, it should be pointed out that S. 1363 is rather limited in its present form. It applies, in the first place, only to *delivery via the U.S. postal service* (not UPS, or over-the-counter sales); and, in the second place, affects only those states *which by state statute* (author's emphasis) prohibit "manufacturing, selling, carrying, or possessing such dangerous martial arts weapons." (S. 1363 amending 13 U.S.C. 1716 (h)(l)(B))

Note here that S. 1363 could easily be amended to ban the nunchaku, shuriken and manrikigusari. Wait until some senator's kid gets a shuriken in the forehead and see how fast the legislative process can work.

Now, on to the nunchaku, shuriken and manrikigusari, weapons so frightening that the august United States Senate checks them out.

Nunchaku

It was noted in testimony before the Senate Subcommittee that a nunchaku can whirl at 100 mph, make coconuts explode like grenades, and when used like a nutcracker "can permanently rearrange an upper vertebra."

The nunchaku is defined in S. 1363 as "consisting of two sticks of wood, plastic, or metal connected at one end by a length of rope, chain, wore, or leather."

Questions have been raised as to this broad definition. For example, as attorney Stephen P. Halbrook brought out during the Senate hearing, "The nunchaku, the way you define it, would include a jump rope...anything can be used as a weapon."

Opinions from two state courts were cited to the Senate Judiciary Committee in support of the nunchaku as a lawful and socially acceptable device. The Hawaii Supreme Court used the following language:

Today, nunchaku sticks are widely used in the martial arts to build up dexterity, mind and body coordination, and aids in developing a larger sphere of consciousness around an individual. We believe that nunchaku sticks, as used in the martial arts, are socially acceptable and lawful behavior (author's emphasis). *(State v. Mulifu)*

On the other side of the continent, the Pennsylvania Supreme Court reached a similar conclusion with similar language:

There is no doubt that the nunchaku can be used offensively, as can a golf club or a baseball bat, to inflict serious injury. However, a student, or instructor of the martial arts, would have occasion to use the nunchaku in the peaceful practice of karate exercises. The martial arts are practiced by many citizens of this commonwealth as a sport and exercise. (Commonwealth v. Adams)

According to historical accounts, the nunchaku was once no more than an everyday Okinawan farm implement—a rice beater. It was improvised to become a lethal weapon by an underground resistance movement committed to defying their Japanese occupiers.

The California Legislature defines the nunchaku as "an instrument consisting of two or more sticks, clubs, bars or rods to be used as handles, connected by a rope, cord, wire or chain, in the design of a weapon used in...karate." These nunchaku can generate 1,600 pounds of pressure at the point of impact. Since human bones break at about eight and a half pounds of pressure, the capacity nunchaku hold for serious injury is considerable.

The following states regulate conduct with the nunchaku:

Arizona
California
Connecticut
Illinois
Kentucky
Maryland
Massachusetts
Nevada
New York
North Dakota
Virginia
Washington
West Virginia
and Rhode Island by implication

Shuriken

The shuriken (shaken) finds its origins in the fog and night of feudal Japan, where *ninja* roamed. These "death stars" are either thrown or used like a knife. Most of the martial arts store-variety shuriken are, in fact, far from deadly. They are merely trinkets. Sure, they might put an eye out—but "deadly"? Certainly not in the same league as a Saturday night special. Nevertheless, most jurisdictions that legislate martial arts weapons also legislate shuriken.

The following states regulate conduct with the shuriken:

Arkansas
California
Connecticut
Indiana

Kentucky
Maryland
Massachusetts
Nevada
New York
North Dakota
Virginia
Washington
and Rhode Island by implication

The shuriken is defined in S. 1363 as "a starlike object intended to injure a person when thrown." The Judiciary Committee heard testimony about a shuriken that was "teflon-coated so it would penetrate a bullet-proof vest," and a shuriken that was "aimed for the carotid artery, to slice the side of your throat, so you would bleed to death."

As with the nunchaku, threshold definitional problems arose. It was pointed out to the Judiciary Committee that the shuriken is commonly defined as "a knife made for throwing... The hilt and blade are forged in one piece." So are regular throwing knives and even tomahawks covered?

It is interesting to note that the shuriken is known by no less than ten different names among state statutes:

(1) "Chinese throwing star"—Indiana
(2) "throwing star"—Arkansas, Kansas, North Dakota
(3) "shuriken"—California
(4) "Chinese star"—Connecticut
(5) "death star"—Kentucky
(6) "star knife"—Maryland
(7) "trefoil"—Nevada
(8) "kung fu star"—New York
(9) "throwing star or oriental dart"—Virginia
(10) "ninja star"—Puerto Rico

Witness J. Bruce Voyles made an interesting observation. He testified that "owning throwing stars is little different than owning darts! I feel certain that there are more injuries from darts thrown by intoxicated bar patrons than there are from martial arts weapons."

Ninja master Stephen Hayes, through written testimony, observed that the shuriken is not designed as a "killing weapon" since its points are too short to penetrate for a killing cut.

The prize for the most original criticism goes to attorney Stephen P. Halbrook, who observed that "The First Amendment guarantees of free expression and religion will be affected by a ban on metal shapes such as the Star of David or Christmas stars. Will a metal star be prohibited if the word 'ninja' is stamped on it, but not if it contains a religious message? Will the government judge free speech content?"

Manrikigusari

Lastly, the manrikigusari is defined in S. 1363 as simply a weapon "consisting of a length of chain having weighted ends."

Both Halbrook and Hayes pointed out that this was the perfect definition of a tow chain. Halbrook also noted that the manrikigusari was not developed by the bugaboo ninjas, but by the Japanese police as a purely defensive weapon.

Actually, it goes back further than that. According to historical accounts:

According to the written records of Masaki-ryu, the founder of the manrikigusari and the person chiefly responsible for its development is Dannoshin Toshimitsu Masaki—one of the most famous and skilled swordsmen of his day.

While assigned as Head Sentry for the main gate of Edo (Tokyo) Castle, it was the responsibility of Masaki and his disciples to guard against the intrusion of bandits, hoodlums, or otherwise insane persons. It was at that time that Masaki became aware and gravely concerned that should an attempt be made to breach the gate, it would certainly result in the heavy flow of blood.

Masaki's convictions dictated that such bloody battles should not take place before such a famous and important gate. He felt that a sword should never be unsheathed at such a sacred place nor should it be soiled with blood, yet the castle gate must be defended at all costs. For some time to follow, Masaki gave considerable thought to what type of weapon would be most appropriate. For reasons known only to himself, he decided that the use of the chain in some form would be most suitable for defending not only against unarmed enemies, but also those armed with sticks, swords, and other types of weapons. As a result, he constructed many kinds of chain weapons with iron weights attached to them—this was the birth of the manrikigusari. (These events are alleged to have occurred about two hundred years ago.) (Ninja Weapons, Charles Gruzanski, 1967).

In another book, Gruzanski continues:

...Before Masaki presented the manrikigusari techniques, he always instructed the receiver that the manrikigusari was not meant for unnecessary fighting and that it should be used only for right. Should it be used for wrongdoing, Masaki warned that that person would destroy himself physically and spiritually. (Spike And Chain, C. Gruzanski, 1968).

Reader, beware. Within statutes in Arizona, California, Nevada, Rhode Island, Washington and West Virginia, the nunchaku is defined in such a way that the manrikigusari could be included in the same definition. However, a strong defense could be made that in light of their varied historical origins and usage (nunchaku primarily strikes while manrikigusari primarily entangles), a deadly weapons statute specifically banning or restricting the use of nunchaku might be held *not* to cover manrikigusari by implication of law because of the statutory interpretation doctrine of *expressio unius est exclusio alterius* (explicit expression of one (weapon) excludes other (weapons) not mentioned).

Is There A Need For Martial Arts Weapon Legislation?

Within FBI crime statistics, weapon assaults are not broken down into those which do and those which do not involve martial arts weapons. No neat case can be made regarding mayhem attributable to the nunchaku, shuriken or manrikigusari. As Jonathan Reinschreiber brought out in testimony before the Senate Subcommittee:

Currently there is no source of information concerning the use of martial arts implements in the commission of violent crime. The Federal Bureau of Investigation compiles all violent crime into its annual 'Uniform Crime Report, Crime in the United States.' This report is compiled from questionnaires mailed out to state, county and local law enforcement agencies. There is no place on this questionnaire for reporting the use of martial arts implements. The questionnaire does request information on the use of weapons divided into eleven categories. Two of these weapon-type categories are one 'cutting or stabbing instruments' (i.e., knives, kitchen cutlery, screwdrivers, ice picks, etc.), and 'blunt objects' (i.e., hammers, clubs, iron pipes, baseball bats, etc.). Because of the nature of martial arts implements, it can be assumed that they are included in these two categories. (An Analysis of the Statistical Necessity for the Federal Control of Martial Arts Implements)

The Reinschreiber analysis was corroborated by a November 8, 1985 letter from Steven R. Schlesinger, the director of the Bureau of Justice Statistics at the U.S. Department of Justice. He admitted, "It is true that detailed statistics about criminal martial arts weapons use are almost nonexistent." However, Mr. Schlesinger also noted that this "does not mean that such (martial arts) weapons are not used to commit a substantial number of crimes." The Schlesinger letter, which was included in the transcript of the Judiciary Committee hearing, reasoned that the data had not been collected for the following reasons: First, the two National Crime Indexes, the FBI's Uniform Crime Reports, and the Bureau of Justice Statistics National Crime Survey were "not designed to measure unusual types of crime or their characteristics."

Second, data would be inaccurate "because most victims, as well as many law enforcement personnel, would be unfamiliar with such foreign weapons." For example, nunchaku might be identified as a stick and chain.

Third, persons attacked with martial arts weapons might be involved in illegal activities and would therefore not report the incident.

However, some statistical evidence can be gleaned from a survey conducted on "weapon acquisition and use among the incarcerated felon population." At the request of the office of S. 1363 co-sponsor Senator Kennedy, Dr. James D. Wright, professor of sociology at the University of Massachusetts at Amhurst, submitted information to the Judiciary Committee regarding the use of martial arts weapons among felons. His data was based on a questionnaire given to 1,874 men doing felony time in ten state prisons across the nation.

The statistics are quite interesting. 1,270 men committed assault. Of these, although 817 used a weapon, only 29 used a martial arts weapon. This is less than 2.3 percent. 1,261 men committed burglary. Of these, although 545 were armed with a weapon, only 11 used a martial arts weapon. This is barely 2 percent. There were 893 drug dealers. 532 were armed with a weapon, and only 19 had a martial arts weapon (3.5 percent). Of 907 robberies committed, 767 robbers were armed with weapons and in only *nine* instances were these martial arts weapons (1.2 percent). As for homicides, 225 turned up on the survey, and in only *two* cases (less than 1 percent) was a martial arts weapon used. Furthermore, there is no data regarding whether these weapons were obtained via the U.S. Postal Service! As Professor Wright concluded in his closing paragraph:

The survey contains no information on how these men obtained their martial arts weapons, so I cannot estimate the fraction obtained via mail orders. Also, no earlier survey of comparable scope and detail exists, so it cannot be said whether the use of martial arts weapons by felons is increasing or decreasing. The data from this survey do confirm, however, that at least some felons (a small fraction of the total, to be sure) do commit crimes with these weapons.

The Consumer Product Safety Commission estimated that, in the last five years, 100,000 injuries caused by practicing the martial arts were treated in emergency rooms. More than one witness pointed out that these were *sports* injuries, not weapons injuries. Thus, they were irrelevant to the Committee's consideration.

Without a doubt, the most exhaustive and painstaking statistical survey put before the Judiciary Committee had to be the 24-page document titled "An Analysis of the Statistical Necessity for the Federal Control of Martial Arts Implements" prepared by Jonathan Reinschreiber. After studying a series of charts and graphs and a survey of trends, and after doing some hard-core analysis, Mr. Reinschreiber concluded, "There is no evidence that the availability of martial arts implements has contributed to increases in violent crimes or in the commission of violent crimes by minors."

Mr. Reinschreiber's last remark to the committee was, "Gentlemen, certainly there are more important issues to be placed before the Senate."

But proponents of the legislation got their licks in as well. Deputy Assistant United States Attorney General Victoria Toensing testified that "state and local police officers attending the FBI Academy...have reported to the Bureau staff that there is an increasing use of martial arts weapons by street gangs." This was confirmed by Boston Police Department spokesperson Joseph C. Carter, who testified, "...Of the 3,000 or so arrests for dangerous weapons (in Boston, 1984)...a majority of those weapons are martial arts-type weapons, be they shurikens, the nunchakus, or the manrikigusari..."

Members of the organizations National Eye Trauma System and the National Society to Prevent Blindness applauded S. 1363 in letters they submitted to the Judiciary Committee.

What If S. 1363 Became Law?

The proposed federal legislation would apply only to the delivery of martial arts weapons via the U.S. Postal Service to those states which "prohibit manufacturing, selling, carrying or possessing such dangerous martial arts weapons." In the first place, as observed by U.S. Postal Service Assistant Chief Inspector Jack E. Swagerty, "Less than a third of the states at the present time have laws covering martial arts weapons."

Attorney Karl Duff led the Senate Subcommittee through a state-by-state survey. In an elaborate chart provided to the Judiciary Committee, the law of twelve states was set forth. By studying the chart, it was noted that some states, such as Kentucky, merely prohibit *concealing* deadly weapons, but in no wise *bans* the weapons (as required before S. 1363 would click into operation).

When Will It Become Unlawful To Transform
Hands and Feet Into Deadly Weapons?

Those who fail to realize that hands and feet can be deadly weapons are invited to view the film of Mas Oyama killing a young, healthy bull with his bare hands. The bull's body was so mutilated that the butcher refused it. And does anyone doubt the potentially possible brutalness of the ninja hands and feet?

Here's the rhetorical question of the month: who wouldn't rather face some meek-looking kid, "heavily armed" with a nunchaku, a manrikigusari and even a shuriken or two, than an unarmed black belt? This writer would take his chances with the kid any day of the week.

The venerable Jhoon Rhee, martial artist of forty years and special consultant to the President's Council on Physical Fitness, testified before the Senate Judiciary Committee both orally and in writing. He eloquently and simply raised the question: "How do I know Senator Kennedy will not introduce another bill to ban martial arts, for the same reason of this bill?" The logic is compelling. Have you heard about the camel who politely asked if he could put his nose in the tent? Next came the head. Then the shoulders. And before the tent occupants knew it, the tent covered the camel like a blanket and they were out in the cold.

Fortunately, S. 1363 went from the Senate Judiciary Committee to "general orders" status. "Congress found out what a formidable force the martial arts community was." However, in its current status, S. 1363 is in a state of "suspended animation." It could rear its ugly head again.

Conclusion

Rainbow Publications Inc. publisher, Michael James made an excellent and original point when testifying before the Senate Judiciary Committee. He brought out that the martial arts are in a *developmental* stage, particularly in terms of weaponry, and made the analogy to fencing.

The similarities of the development of these items in sport are not unlike the sport of fencing. Fencing historically taught the art of dueling. Since the practice of dueling has been dropped, fencing has developed into a sophisticated sport now included in the Olympics. The tools of the sport, the foil and various swords, are now considered sports implements... The martial arts items are in a similar stage of development and can be considered the equivalent of fencing swords. It should be taken into consideration also that there are rules of competition which includes no contact and stress form and skill only. We find that the similarities between classical fencing and the martial arts items to be uncanny.

"Freestyle shuriken throwing" in the 2000 Olympics? Could be!

If federal or state law someday banned martial arts weapons, this would result in the creation of a new class of weapons just as surely as night follows day. Can you imagine the American *dojo* in 2001, requiring that one is proficient in the "tire tool" and "pick ax" to achieve the coveted black belt? Ludicrous? No doubt the Okinawan farmer probably never considered his lowly farm tool to be a "coconut-exploding weapon" before the occupying Japanese military took his sword away. With weapons, as generally with life, necessity is the mother of invention!

To conclude: deadly martial arts weapons laws cover many things, such as:

—when you can possess martial arts weapons;

—whether you can manufacture or sell a martial arts weapon;

—whether you can conceal these weapons;

—and how you may not brandish certain oriental weapons.

This chapter intends to show you where some of the legal land-mines lay. It is possible that other statutes not mentioned in this chapter could govern your situation. *Here's the best legal advice I can give you: consult a lawyer in your jurisdiction should legal questions arise.*

For simplicity, the following statutes have referred to legislative codes. For example, at the end of "Kentucky" you see the number 500.080. This is shorthand for K.R.S. 500.080 (Kentucky Revised Statutes). Each state, by definition, can have only one set of statutes.

Special thanks go to Murray Porath, Kathy Munroe and Tom Jackson, whose efforts in the law library helped produce these updated state-by-state statutes. (Note: The statues cited may have been amended since publication of this book. Use citations to see if the law's changed in your state.)

DEADLY WEAPON STATUTES

ALABAMA

Except as otherwise provided in this Code, a person who carries concealed about his person a bowie knife or knife or instrument of the kind or description or a pistol or firearm of any other kind or an air gun shall, on conviction, be find not less than $50 nor more than $500, and may also be imprisoned in the county jail or sentenced to hard labor for the county for not more than six months. (13A-11-50)

Anyone who carries concealed about his person brass knuckles, slingshots or other weapons of like kind or description shall, on conviction, be fined not less than $50 nor more than $500, and may also be imprisoned in the county jail or sentenced to hard labor for the county for not more than six months. (13A-11-53)

Any person who carries a rifle or shotgun walking cane shall, on conviction, be fined not less than $500 nor more than $1,000, and be imprisoned in the penitentiary not less than two years. (13A-11-54)

ALASKA

...As used in this section, "prohibited weapon" means any explosive, incendiary, or noxious gas; mine or device that is designed, made, or adapted for the purpose of inflicting serious physical injury or death; rocket, other than an emergency flare, having a propellant charge of more than four ounces; bomb; grenade; device designed, made or adapted to muffle the report of a firearm; metal knuckles; switchblade or gravity knife; firearm that is capable of shooting more than one shot automatically, without manual reloading, by a single function of the trigger; or rifle with a barrel length of less than 16 inches, shotgun with a barrel length of less than 18 inches, or firearm made from a rifle or shotgun which, as modified, has an overall length of less than 26 inches. (11.61.200)

ARIZONA

"Deadly weapon" means anything designed for lethal use. The term includes a firearm. "Prohibited weapon" means, but does not include, fireworks imported, distributed or used in compliance with state laws or local ordinances, any propellant, propellant actuated devices or propellant actuated industrial tools which are manufactured, imported or distributed for their intended purposes or a device which is commercially manufactured primarily for the purpose of illumination, any: (A) Explosive, incendiary or poison gas; (i) bomb; (ii) grenade; (iii) rocket having a propellant charge of more than four ounces; (iv) mine. (B)

Device designed, made or adapted to muffle the report of a firearm; or (C) Firearm that is capable of shooting more than one shot automatically, without manual reloading, by a single function of the trigger; or (D) Rifle with a barrel length of less than eighteen inches, or any firearm made from a rifle or shotgun which, as modified, has an overall length of less than 26 inches; or (E) Instrument, including a nunchaku, that consists of two or more sticks, clubs, bars or rods to be used as handles, connected by a rope, cord, wire or chain, in the design of a weapon used in connection with the practice of a system of self-defense; or (F) Breakable container which contains a flammable liquid with a flash point of 150 degrees Fahrenheit or less and has a wick or similar device capable of being ignited; or (G) Combination of parts or materials designed and intended for the use in making or converting a device into an item set forth in subdivision (A) or (F) of this paragraph. The items as set forth in subdivision (A), (B), (C) and (D) of this paragraph shall not include such firearms or devices registered in the national firearms registry and transfer records of the United States Treasury Department or any firearm which has been classified as a curio or relic by the United States Treasury Department. (13.3101)

ARKANSAS

(a) A person commits the offense of criminal use of prohibited weapons if, except as authorized by law, he uses, possesses, makes, repairs, sells or otherwise deals in any bomb, machine gun, sawed-off shotgun, firearm specially made or specially adapted for silent discharge, metal knuckles, or other implement for the infliction of serious physical injury or death which serves no common lawful purpose. (5-73-104)

(a) A person commits the offense of carrying a weapon if he possesses a handgun, knife, or club on or about his person, in a vehicle occupied by him, or otherwise readily available for use with a purpose to employ it as a weapon against a person... (2) "Knife" means any bladed hand instrument that is capable of inflicting serious physical injury or death by cutting or stabbing. It includes a dirk, sword or spear in a cane, razor, ice pick, and a throwing star, switchblade, and butterfly knife. (5-73-120)

CALIFORNIA

Certain firearms, ammunition, explosive substances, metal plate weapons, etc.; manufacture, import, sale, etc. prohibited; exceptions; definitions: (a) Any person in this state who manufactures or causes to be manufactured, imports into the state, keeps for sale, or offers or exposes for sale, or who gives, lends, or possesses any cane gun or wallet gun, any plastic firearm, any firearm which is not immediately recognizable as a firearm, any camouflaging firearm container, any ammunition which contains or consists of any flechette dart, any bullet containing or carrying an explosive agent, any ballistic knife, any multiburst trigger activator, any nunchaku, any short-barreled shotgun, any short-barreled rifle, any metal knuckles, any belt buckle knife, any leaded cane, any zip gun, any shuriken, any unconventional pistol, any lipstick case knife, any cane sword, any shobi-zue, any air gauge knife, any writing pen knife, or any instrument or weapon of the kind commonly known as a blackjack, slungshot, billy, sandclub, sap, or sandbag, or who carries concealed upon his or her person any explosive substance, other than fixed ammunition or who carries concealed upon his or her person any dirk or dagger, is guilty of a felony, and upon conviction shall be punishable by imprisonment in a county jail not exceeding one year or in the state prison... (b) Subdivision (a) does not apply to any of the following: ...(3) The possession of a nunchaku on the premises of a school which holds a regulatory or business license and teaches the arts of self-defense. (4) The manufacture of a nunchaku for sale to, or the sale of a nunchaku to, a school which holds a regulatory or business license and teaches the arts of self-defense... (3) As used in this section, a "nunchaku" means an instrument consisting of two or more sticks, clubs, bars or rods to be used as handles, connected by a rope, cord, wire, or chain, in the design of a weapon to be used in connection with the practice of a system of self-defense such as karate... (11) As used in this section, a "shuriken" means any instrument, without handles, consisting of a metal plate having three or more radiating points with one or more sharp edges and designed in the shape of a polygon, trefoil, cross, star, diamond, or other geometric shape for use as a weapon for throwing... (16) as used in this section, a 'shobi-zue" means a staff, crutch, stick, rod, or pole concealing a knife or blade within it which may be exposed by a flip of the wrist or by a mechanical action. (12020)

COLORADO

Definitions. (1) As used in this article, unless the context other-wise requires: (a) "Blackjack" includes any billy, sandclub, sandbag, or other hand-operated striking weapon consisting, at the striking end, of an encased piece of lead or other heavy substance and, at the handle end, a strap or springy shaft which increases the force of impact. (b) "Bomb" means any explosive or incendiary device or molotov cocktail as defined in 9-7-103, C.R.S, which is not specifi-cally designed for lawful and legitimate use in the hands of its pos-sessor. (c) "Firearm silencer" means any instrument, attachment, weapon, or appliance for causing the firing of any gun, revolver, pis-tol, or other firearm to be silent or intended to lessen or muffle the noise of the firing of any such weapon. (d) "Gas gun" means a device designed for projecting gas-filled projectiles which release their con-tents after having been projected from the device and includes pro-jectiles designed for use in such a device. (e) "Gravity knife" means any knife that has a blade released from the handle or sheath thereof by the force of gravity or the application of centrifugal force, that when released is locked in place by means of a button, spring, lever, or other device. (f) "Knife" means any dagger, dirk, knife, or stiletto blade over three and one-half inches in length, or any other danger-ous instrument capable of inflicting cutting, stabbing, or tearing wounds, but does not include a hunting or fishing knife carried for sports use. The issue that a knife is a hunting or fishing knife must be raised as an affirmative defense. (g) "Machine gun" means any firearm, whatever its size and usual designation, that shoots auto-matically more than one shot, without manual reloading by a single function of the trigger. (h) "Short rifle" means a rifle having a barrel less than sixteen inches. (i) "Short shotgun" means a shotgun having a barrel or barrels less than eighteen inches long or an overall length of less than twenty-six inches. (j) "Switchblade knife" means any

119

knife, the blade of which opens automatically by hand pressure applied to a button, spring, or other device in its handle. (2) It shall be an affirmative defense to any provision of this article that the act was committed by a peace officer in the lawful discharge of his duties. (18-12-101)

Definitions. (1) (a) "Ballistic knife" means any knife that has a blade which is forcefully projected from the handle by means of a spring-loaded device or explosive charge. (a.5) "Blackjack" means any billy, sandclub, sandbag, or other hand-operated striking weapon consisting, at the striking end, of an encased piece of lead or other heavy substance and, at the handle end, a strap or springy shaft which increases the force of impact. (b) "Bomb" means any explosive or incendiary device or molotov cocktail as defined in section 9-8-103, C.R.S. or any chemical device which causes or can cause an explosion, which is not specifically designed for lawful and legitimate use in the hands of its possessor. (i.5) "Stun gun" means a device capable of temporarily immobilizing a person by the infliction of an electrical charge. (18-12-101)

CONNECTICUT

Definitions. (6) "Deadly weapon" means any weapon, whether loaded or unloaded, from which a shot may be discharged, or a switchblade knife, gravity knife, billy, blackjack, bludgeon, or metal knuckles... (7) "Dangerous instrument" means any instrument, article or substance which, under the circumstances in which it is used or attempted or threatened to be used, is capable of causing death or serious physical injury, and includes a "vehicle" as that term is defined in this section... (21) "Martial arts weapon" means a nunchaku, kama, karsari-fundo, octagon sai, tonfa or chinese star. (53a-3)

DELAWARE

When used in this Criminal Code: (5) "Deadly weapon" includes a firearm, as defined in paragraph (9) of this section, a bomb, a knife of any sort (other than an ordinary pocket knife carried in a closed position), switchblade knife, billy, blackjack, bludgeon, metal knuckles, sling-shot, razor, bicycle chain or ice pick or any dangerous instrument, as defined in paragragh (4) of this section... Barbell and bowling ball not "deadly weapon(s)".—A barbell and bowling ball are items of common usage, and while they may become deadly instrumentalities, they are not deadly weapons; they are not among the items listed in the statute, nor do they bear any similarity to these items. (222)

FLORIDA

Definitions. (3)(a) "Concealed weapon" means any dirk, metallic knuckles, slungshot, billie, tear gas gun, chemical weapon or device, or other deadly weapon carried on or about a person in such a manner as to conceal the weapon from ordinary sight of another person. (790.001)

GEORGIA

(1) "Dangerous weapon" means any weapon commonly known as a "rocket launcher," "bazooka," or "recoilless rifle" which fires explosive or nonexplosive rockets designed to injure or kill personnel or destroy heavy armor, or similar weapon used for such purpose. The term shall also mean a weapon commonly known as "mortar" which fires high explosive from a metallic cylinder and which is commonly used by the armed forces as an antipersonnel weapon or similar weapon used for such purpose. The term shall also mean a weapon commonly known as a "hand grenade" or other similar weapon which is designed to explode and injure personnel or similar weapon used for such purpose. (16.11.121)

HAWAII

Deadly weapons; prohibitions penalty: (a) Any person not authorized by law, who carries concealed upon one's person or within any vehicle used or occupied by the person, or who is found armed with any dirk, dagger, blackjack, slug shot, billy, metal knuckles, pistol, or other deadly or dangerous weapon, shall be guilty of a misdemeanor. Any such person may be immediately arrested without warrant by any sheriff, police officer, or other officer or person. Any weapon, above enumerated, shall, upon conviction of the one carrying or possessing same under this section, be summarily destroyed by the chief of police or sheriff. (b) Whoever knowingly possesses or intentionally uses or threatens to use a deadly or dangerous weapon

while engaged in the commission of a crime shall be guilty of a class
C felony. (134-51)

IDAHO

Concealed and dangerous weapons—Possession and exhibition—Sale to minors: —If any person, excepting officials of a county, officials of the state of Idaho, officials of the United States, peace
officers, guards of any jail, or any officer of any express company on
duty, shall carry concealed upon or about his person, any dirk, dirk
knife, bowie knife, dagger, sling shot, pistol, revolver, gun or any
other deadly or dangerous weapon within the limits or confines of
any city, town or village, or in any public assembly, or in any min-
ing, lumbering, logging, railroad or other construction camp, public
conveyance or on public highways within the state of Idaho, shall, in
the presence of one (1) or more persons, exhibit any deadly or dangerous weapon in a rude, angry or threatening manner, or shall have
or carry such weapons upon or about his person when intoxicated or
under the influence of intoxicating drinks, or shall, directly or indirectly, sell or deliver, loan or barter to any minor under the age of sixteen (16) years any such weapon without the consent of the parent
or guardian of such minor, he shall, upon conviction, be punished by
a fine of not less than $25 nor more than $200, and by imprisonment in the county jail for a period of not less than twenty (20) days
nor more than ninety (90) days provided, however, that any person
shall be allowed to carry any of the above weapons in the places mentioned above on securing a permit from the sheriff of the county after
satisfying the sheriff of the necessity therefor. (18-3302)

ILLINOIS

Unlawful use of weapons: (a) A person commits the offense of
unlawful use of weapons when he knowingly: (1) Sells, manufactures, purchases, possesses or carries any bludgeon, blackjack, slungshot, sandclub, sandbag, metal knuckles, throwing star, or any knife,
commonly referred to as a switchblade knife, which has a blade that
opens automatically by hand pressure applied to a button, spring or
other device in the handle of the knife, or a ballistic knife, which is
a device that propels a knifelike blade as a projectile by means of a

coil spring, elastic material or compressed gas; or (2) Carries or possesses with the intent to use the same unlawfully against another, a dagger, dirk, billy, dangerous knife, razor, stiletto, broken bottle or other piece of glass, stun gun or taser or any other dangerous or deadly weapon or instrument of like character; or (3) Carries on or about his person or in any vehicle, a tear gas gun projector or bomb or any kind object containing noxious liquid gas or substance, other than an object containing a non-lethal noxious liquid gas or substance designed solely for personal defense carried by a person 18 years of age or older; or (4) Carries or possesses in any vehicle or concealed on or about his person, except when on his land or in his own abode or fixed place of business any pistol, revolver, stun gun or taser or other firearm; or (5) Sets a spring gun; or (6) Possesses any device or attachment of any kind designed, used or intended for use in silencing the report of any firearm; or (7) Sells, manufactures, purchases, possesses or caries a machine gun, which shall be defined for the purposes of this subsection as any weapon, which shoots, is designed to shoot, or can be readily restored to shoot, automatically more than one shot without manually reloading by a single function of the trigger, including the frame or receiver of any such weapon, or sells, manufactures, purchases, possesses, or carries any combination of parts designed or intended for use in converting any weapon into a machine gun, or any combination of parts from which a machine gun can be assembled if such parts are in the possession or under the control of a person, or any rifle having one or more barrels less than 16 inches in length or a shotgun having one or more barrels less than 18 inches in length or any weapon made from a rifle or shotgun, whether by alteration, modification, or otherwise, if such a weapon as modified has an overall length of less than 26 inches or any bomb, bombshell, grenade, bottle or other container containing an explosive substance of over one-quarter ounce for like purposes, such as, but not limited to, black powder bombs and Molotov cocktails or artillery projectiles; or (8) Carries or possesses any firearm, stun gun or taser or other deadly weapon in any place which is licensed to sell intoxicating beverages, or at any public gathering held pursuant to a license issued by any governmental body or any public gathering at which an admission is charged, excluding a place where a showing, demonstration or lecture involving the exhibition of unloaded firearms is conducted; or (9) Carries or possesses in a vehicle or on or about his person any pistol, revolver, stun gun or taser or firearm or ballistic knife, when he is hooded, robed or masked in such manner as to conceal his identity; or (10) Carries or possesses on or about his person, upon any public street, alley, or other public lands within the corporate limits of a city, village or incorporated town, except when an invitee thereon or therein, for the purpose of display of such weapon or the lawful commerce in weapons, or except when his land or his own abode or fixed place of business, any pistol, revolver, stun gun or taser or other firearm. A "stun gun or taser," as used in this paragraph (a) means (i) any device which is powered by electrical charging units, such as, batteries, and which fires one or several barbs attached to a length of wire and which, upon hitting a human, can send out a current capable of disrupting the person's nervous system in such a manner as to render him incapable of normal functioning or (ii) any device which is powered by electrical charging units, such as batteries, and which, upon contact with a human or clothing worn by a human, can send out current capable of disrupting the person's nervous system in such a manner as to render him incapable of normal functioning; or (11) Sells, manufactures or purchases any explosive bullet. For purposes of this paragraph (a) "explosive bullet" means the projectile portion of an ammunition cartridge which contains or carries an explosive charge which will explode upon contact with the flesh of a human or an animal. "Cartridge" means a tubular metal case having a projectile affixed at the front thereof and a cap or primer at the rear end thereof, with the propellant contained in such tube between the projectile cap; or (12) Carries or possesses on about his person any bludgeon, blackjack, slingshot, sandclub, sandbag, metal knuckles, switchblade knife, ballistic knife, tear gas gun projector bomb or any object containing noxious liquid gas, pistol or revolver or other firearm, bomb, grenade, bottle or other container containing an explosive substance of over one-quarter ounce or cartridge while in the building or on the grounds of any elementary or secondary school, community college, college or university. This paragraph (12) shall not apply to law enforcement officers or security officers of such school, college or university, nor to students carrying or possessing firearms for use in training courses, parades, hunting, target shooting on school ranges, or otherwise with the consent of school authorities and which firearms are transported, unloaded and enclosed in a suitcase, box or transportation package... (c) Exemptions: Crossbows, Common or Compound bows and Underwater Spearguns are exempted from the definition of ballistic knife as defined in paragraph (1) of subsection (a) of this Section. (24-1)

INDIANA

Knife with automatically opening blade prohibited.—It is a class B misdemeanor for a person to manufacture, possess, display, offer, sell, lend, give away, or purchase any knife with a blade that opens automatically by hand pressure applied to a button, spring, or other device in the handle of the knife. (35-57-5-2)

Exposing or offering knucks, slingshot or billy for sale prohibited.—It is a class C infraction for a person to expose or offer for sale any knucks, slingshot, or billy. (35-47-5-3)

Dealing in sawed-off shotgun prohibited.—(a) A person who: (1) Manufactures; (2) Causes to be manufactured; (3) Imports into Indiana; (4) Keeps for sale; (5) Offers or exposes for sale; or (6) Gives, lends, or possesses; any sawed-off shotgun commits dealing in a sawed-off shotgun, a class D felony. (b) The presence of a weapon referred to in subsection (a) in a motor vehicle, as defined under IC 9-1-1-2 except for school buses and a vehicle operated in the transportation of passengers by a common carrier, as defined in IC 8-2-7-2, creates an inference that such weapon is in the possession of the persons occupying the motor vehicle. However, the inference does not apply to all the persons occupying the motor vehicle if the weapon is found upon, or under the control of, one of the occupants... (35-47-5-4)

Use of armor-piercing handgun ammunition prohibited— Exception.—(a) As used in this section, "armor-piercing handgun ammunition" means a cartridge that: (1) Can be fired in a handgun; and (2) Will, upon firing, expel a projectile that has a metal core and an outer coating of plastic. (b) A person who knowingly or intentionally: (1) Manufactures; (2) Possesses; (3) Transfers possesion of; or (4) Offers to transfer possession of; armor-piercing handgun ammunition commits a Class C felony. (c) This section does not apply to nylon-coated ammunition, plastic shot capsules, or ammunition designed to be used in rifles or shotguns. (d) This section does not apply to a law enforcement officer who is acting in the course of the officer's official duties or to a person who manufactures or imports for sale or sells armor-piercing handgun ammunition to a law enforcement agency. (35-47-5-11)

Manufacture, sale or possession of Chinese throwing star.—(a) A person who: (1) Manufactures; (2) Causes to be manufactured; (3) Imports into Indiana; (4) Keeps for sale; (5) Offers or exposes for sale; or (6) Gives, lends, or possesses; a Chinese throwing star commits a Class C misdemeanor. (b) As used in this section, "Chinese throwing star" means a throwing knife, throwing-iron, or other knifelike weapon with blades set at different angles. (35-47-5-12)

IOWA

Offensive weapons. An offensive weapon is any device or instrumentality of the following types: 1. A machine gun. A machine gun is a firearm which shoots or is designed to shoot more than one shot, without manual reloading, by a single function of the trigger. 2. A short-barreled rifle or short-barreled shotgun. A short-barreled rifle or short-barreled shotgun is a rifle with a barrel or barrels less than 16 inches in length or a shotgun with a barrel or barrels less than 18 inches in length, as measured from the face of the closed holt or standing breech to the muzzle, or any rifle or shotgun with an overall length less than 26 inches. (8) Any weapon other than a shotgun or muzzle loading rifle, cannon, pistol, revolver or musket, which fires or can be made to fire a projectile by the explosion of a propellant charge, which has a barrel or tube with the bore of more than six-tenths of an inch in diameter, or the ammunition or projectile therefor, but not including antique weapons kept for display or lawful shooting. (4) A bomb, grenade, or mine, whether explosive, incendiary, or poison gas; any rocket having a propellant charge of more than four ounces; any missile having an explosive charge of more than one-quarter ounce; or any device similar to any of these. (5) A ballistic knife. A ballistic knife is a knife with a detachable blade which is propelled by a spring-operated mechanism, elastic material, or compressed gas. (6) Any part or combination of parts either designed or intended to be used to convert any device into an offensive weapon as described in subsection 1 to 5 of this section, or to assemble into such an offensive weapon, except magazines or other parts, ammunition, or ammunition components used in common with lawful sporting firearms or parts including but not limited to barrels suitable for refitting to sporting firearms. (7) Any bullet or projectile containing any explosive mixture or chemical compound capable of exploding or detonating prior to or upon impact, or any shotshell or cartridge containing exothermic pyrophoric misch metal as a projectile which is designed to throw or project a flame or fireball to simulate a flamethrower. Notwithstanding section 724.2, no person is authorized to possess in this state a shotshell or cartridge intended to project a flame or fireball of the type described in this section. (8) Any mechanical device specifically constructed and designed so that when attached to a firearm silences, muffles or suppresses the sound when fired. (9) An offensive weapon or part or combination of parts therefor shall not include the following: (a) An antique firearm. An antique firearm is any firearm (including any firearm with a matchlock, flintlock, percussion cap, or similar type of ignition system) manufactured in or before 1898 or any firearm, which is a replica of such a firearm if such replica is not designed or redesigned for using conventional rimfire or centerfire ammunition or which uses only rimfire or centerfire fixed ammunition which is no longer manufactured in the United States and which is not readily available in the ordinary channels of commercial trade. (b) A collector's item. A collector's item is any firearm other than a machine gun that by reason of its date of manufacture, value, design, and other characteristics is not likely to be used as a weapon. The commissioner of public safety shall designate by rule firearms which the commissioner determines to be collector's items and shall revise or update the list of firearms at least annually. (c) Any device which is not designated or redesigned for use as a weapon; any Device which is designed solely for use as signaling, pyrotechnic, line-throwing, safety, or similar device; or any firearm which is unserviceable by reason of being unable to discharge a shot by means of an explosive and is incapable of being readily restored to a firing condition. (724.1)

KANSAS

Unlawful use of weapons. (1) Unlawful use of weapons is knowingly: (a) Selling, manufacturing, purchasing, possessing or carrying any bludgeon, sandclub, metal knuckles or throwing star, or any knife, commonly referred to as a switchblade, which has a blade that opens automatically by hand pressure applied to a button, spring or other device in the handle of the knife, or any knife having a blade that opens or falls or is ejected into position by the force of gravity or by an outward, downward or centrifugal thrust or movement. (h) Carrying concealed on one's person, or possessing with intent to use the same unlawfully against another, a dagger, dirk, billy, blackjack, slung shot, dangerous knife, straight-edged razor, stiletto or any other dangerous or deadly weapon or instrument of like character, except that an ordinary pocketknife with no blade more than four inches in length shall not be construed to be a dangerous knife, or a dangerous or deadly weapon or instrument. (c) Carrying on one's person or in any land, water or air vehicle, with intent to use the same unlawfully, a tear gas or smoke bomb or projector or any object containing a noxious liquid gas or substance. (d) Carrying any pistol, revolver or other firearm concealed on one's person except when on the person's land or in the person's abode or fixed place of business. (e) Setting a spring gun. (f) Possessing any device or attachment of any kind designed, used or intended for use in silencing the report of any firearm. (g) Selling, manufacturing, purchasing, possessing or carrying a shotgun with a barrel less than 18 inches in length or any other firearm designed to discharge or capable of discharging automatically more than once by a single function of the trigger. (h)

Possessing, manufacturing, causing to be manufactured, selling, offering for sale, lending, purchasing or giving away any cartridge which can be fired by a handgun and which has a plastic-coated bullet that has a core of less than 60 percent lead by weight. (21-4201)

KENTUCKY

...(3) "Dangerous instrument" means any instrument, article or substance which, under the circumstances in which it is used, attempted to be used, or threatened to be used, is readily capable of causing death or serious physical injury. (4) "Deadly weapon" means any weapon: (a) Any weapon from which a shot, readily capable of causing death or other serious physical injury, may be charged; or (b) Any knife other than an ordinary pocketknife or hunting knife; or (c) Billy, nightstick, or club; or (d) Blackjack or slapjack; or (e) Nunchaku karate sticks; or (f) Shuriken or death star; or (g) Artificial knuckles made from metal, plastic or other similar hard material. (500.080)

LOUISIANA

...(3) "Dangerous weapon" includes any gas, liquid or other substance or instrumentality, which, in the manner used, is calculated or likely to produce death or great bodily harm. (R.S. 14:1)

MAINE

9. Dangerous weapon. (1) "Use of a dangerous weapon" means the use of a firearm or other weapon, device, instrument, material or substance, whether animate or inanimate, which, in the manner it is used or threatened to be used is capable of producing death or serious bodily injury. (B) "Armed with a dangerous weapon" means in actual possession, regardless of whether the possession is visible or concealed, of: (1) A firearm; (2) Any device designed as a weapon and capable of producing death or serious bodily injury; or (3) Any other device, instrument, material or substance, whether animate or inanimate, which, in the manner it is intended to be used by the actor, is capable of producing or threatening death or serious bodily injury. For purposes of this definition, the intent may be conditional. (C) When used in any other context, "dangerous weapon" means a firearm or any device designed as a weapon and capable of produc-

ing death or serious bodily injury. (D) For purposes of this subsection, a thing presented in a covered or open manner as a dangerous weapon shall be presumed to be a dangerous weapon. (17-A S.2)

MARYLAND

Carrying or wearing concealed weapon; carrying openly with intent to injure; carrying by person under eighteen at night in certain counties. (a) In general.—Every person who shall wear or carry any dirk knife, bowie knife, switchblade knife, star knife, sandclub, metal knuckles, razor, nunchaku or any other dangerous or deadly weapon of any kind, whatsoever (penknives without switchblades and handguns, excepted) concealed upon or about his person, and every person who shall wear or carry any such weapon, chemical mace or tear gas device openly with the intent or purpose of injuring any person in any unlawful manner, shall be guilty of a misdemeanor, and upon conviction, shall be fined not more than $1,000 or be imprisoned in jail, or sentenced to the Maryland Department of Correction for not more than three years, and in case of conviction, if it shall appear from the evidence that such weapon was carried, concealed or openly, with the deliberate purpose of injuring the person or destroying the life of another, the court shall impose the highest sentence of imprisonment prescribed. In Cecil, Arundel, Talbot, Harford, Caroline, Prince George's, Montgomery, St. Mary's, Washington, Worcester, Kent and Baltimore counties it shall also be unlawful and a misdemeanor, punishable as above set forth, for any person under eighteen years of age to carry any dangerous or deadly weapon, other than a handgun, between one hour after sunset and one hour before sunrise, whether concealed or not, except while on a bona fide hunting trip, or except while engaged in or on the way to or returning from a bona fide trap shoot, sport shooting event, or any organized civic or military activity. (b) "Star knife" defined. — As used in this section, a "star knife" is a device used as a throwing weapon, consisting of several sharp or pointed blades arrayed as radially disposed arms about a central disk. (c) "Nunchaku" defined. — As used in this section, a "nunchaku" is a device constructed of two pieces of any substance, including wood, metal, or plastic, connected by any chain, rope, leather or flexible material, and not exceeding 24 inches in length. (S36)

MASSACHUSETTS

Penalty for Unlawfully Carrying Dangerous Weapons, Possessing Machine Gun, etc... (b) Whoever, except as provided by law, carries on his person, or carries on his person or under his control in a vehicle, any stiletto, dagger, or a device or case which enables a knife with a locking blade to be drawn at a locked position, any ballistic knife, or any knife with a detachable blade capable of being propelled by any mechanism, dirk knife, any knife having a double-edged blade, or a switch knife, or any knife having an automatic spring release device by which the blade is released from the handle, having a blade of over one and one-half inches, or a slung shot, blowgun, blackjack, metallic knuckles or knuckles of any substance which could be put to the same use with the same or similar effect as metallic knuckles, nunchaku, zoobow, also known as klackers or kung fu sticks, or any similar weapon consisting of two sticks of wood, plastic or metal connected at one end by a length of rope, chain, wire or leather, a shuriken or any similar pointed starlike object intended to injure a person when thrown, or any armband, made with leather which has metallic spikes, points or studs or any similar device made from any other substance or a cestus or similar material weighted with metal or other substance and worn on the hand, or a manrikigusari or similar length of chain having weighted ends; or whoever, when arrested upon a warrant for an alleged crime, or when arrested while committing a breach or disturbance of the public peace, is armed with or has on his person, or has on his person or under his control in a vehicle, a billy or other dangerous weapon other than those herein mentioned and those mentioned in paragraph (a), shall be punished by imprisonment for not less than two and one-half years nor more than five years in the state prison, or for not less than six months nor more than two and one-half years in a jail or house of correction, except that, if the court finds that the defendant has not been previously convicted of a felony, he may be punished by a fine of not more than fifty dollars or by imprisonment for not more than two and one-half years in a jail or house of correction. (C.269 S10)

Manufacturing, etc., Slung Shot, etc. Whoever manufactures or causes to be manufactured, or sells or exposes for sale, an instrument or weapon of the kind usually known as a dirk knife, a switch knife or any knife having an automatic spring release device by which the blade is released from the handle, having a blade of over one and one-half inches or a device or case which enables a knife with a locking blade to be drawn at a locked position, any ballistic knife, or any knife with a detachable blade capable of being propelled by any mechanism, slung shot, bean blower, sword cane, pistol cane, bludgeon, blackjack, nunchaku, zoobow, also known as klackers or kung fu sticks, or any similar weapon consisting of two sticks of wood, plastic or metal connected at one end by a length of rope, chain, wire or leather, a shuriken or any similar pointed starlike object intended to injure a person when thrown, or a manrikigusari or similar length of chain having weighted ends; or metallic knuckles, shall be punished by a fine of not less than fifty nor more than one thousand dollars or by imprisonment for not more than six months; provided, however, that sling shots may be manufactured and sold to clubs or associations conducting sporting events where such sling shots are used. (C.269, S12)

MICHIGAN

...(1) A person shall not manufacture, sell, offer for sale, or possess any of the following: (a) A machine gun or firearm shoots or is designed to shoot automatically more than one shot without manual reloading, by a single function of the trigger. (b) A muffler or silencer. (c) A bomb or bombshell. (d) A blackjack, slungshot, billy, metallic knuckles, sand club, sand bag, or bludgeon. (e) A device, weapon, cartridge, container, or contrivance designed to render a person temporarily or permanently disabled by the ejection, release, or emission of a gas or other substance. (750.224)

MINNESOTA

...Subd. 6. Dangerous weapon. "Dangerous weapon" means any firearm, whether loaded or unloaded, or any device designed as a weapon and capable of producing death or great bodily harm, or any flammable liquid or other device or instrumentality that, in the manner it is used or intended to be used, is calculated or likely to produce death or great bodily harm. (609.02)

MISSISSIPPI

Deadly weapons; carrying while concealed; use or attempt to use; penalties. (1) Except as otherwise provided in Section 45-9-101, any person who carries, concealed in whole or in part, any bowie knife, dirk knife, butcher knife, switchblade knife, metallic knuckles, blackjack, slingshot, pistol, revolver, or any rifle with a barrel of less than sixteen (16) inches in length, or any shotgun with a barrel of less than eighteen (18) inches in length, machine gun or any fully automatic firearm or deadly weapon, or any muffler or silencer for any firearm, whether or not it is accompanied by a firearm, or uses or attempts to use against another person any imitation firearm, shall upon conviction be punished... (97-37-1)

MISSOURI

Dangerous and concealed weapons, prohibitions concerning—exceptions—penalty. If any person shall carry concealed upon or about his person a dangerous or deadly weapon of any kind or description, or shall go into any church or place where people have assembled for religious worship, or into any school room or place where people are assembled for educational, political, literary or social purposes, or to any election precinct on any election day, or into any courtroom during the sitting of court, or into any other public assemblage of persons met for any lawful purpose other than for militia drill, or meetings called under militia law of this state, having upon or about his person, concealed or exposed, any kind of firearm, bowie knife, springback knife, razor, metal knuckles, billy, sword cane, dirk, dagger, slung shot or other similar deadly weapons or shall, in the presence of one or more persons, exhibit any such weapon in a rude, angry or threatening manner, or shall have any such weapon in his possession when intoxicated, or, directly or indirectly, sell or deliver, loan or barter to any minor any such weapon without the consent of the parent or guardian of such minor... (571.115)

MONTANA

...(71) "Weapon" means any instrument, article, or substance which, regardless of its primary function, is readily capable of being used to produce death or serious bodily injury... (45-2-101)

Definitions. "Concealed weapon" means any weapon mentioned in 45-8-316 through 45-8-318 and 45-8-321 through 45-8-328 that is wholly or partially covered by the clothing or wearing apparel of the person carrying or bearing the weapon, except that for purposes of 45-8-321 through 45-3-328, concealed weapon means a handgun or a knife with a blade 4 or more inches in length that is wholly or partially covered by the clothing or wearing apparel of the person carrying or bearing the weapon. (45-8-315)

Carrying concealed weapons. (1) Every person who carries or bears concealed upon his person a dirk, dagger, pistol, revolver, sling-shot, sword cane, billy, knuckles made of any metal or hard substance, knife having a blade of 4 inches or longer, razor, not including a safety razor, or other deadly weapon shall be punished by a fine not exceeding $500 or imprisonment in the county jail for a period not exceeding 6 months, or both... (45-8-316)

NEBRASKA

...(2) Knife shall mean any dagger, dirk, knife, or stiletto with a blade over three and one-half inches in length, or any other dangerous instrument capable of inflicting cutting, stabbing, or tearing wounds. (3) Knuckles and brass or iron knuckles shall mean any instrument that consists of finger rings or guards made of a hard substance and that is designed, made, or adapted for the purpose of inflicting serious bodily injury or death by striking a person with a fist enclosed in the knuckles. (4) Machine gun shall mean any firearm, whatever its size and usual designation, that shoots automatically more than one shot, without manual reloading, by a single function of the trigger. (5) Short rifle shall mean a rifle having a barrel less than sixteen inches long or an overall length of less than twenty-six inches; and (6) Short shotgun shall mean a shotgun having a barrel or barrels less than eighteen inches long or an overall length of less than twenty-six inches. (28-1201)

Carrying concealed weapon; penalty; affirmative defense. (1) Except as provided in subsection (2) of this section, any person who carries a weapon or weapons concealed on or about his or her person such as a revolver, pistol, bowie knife, dirk or knife with a dirk blade attachment, brass or iron knuckles, or any other deadly weapon commits the offense of carrying a concealed weapon. (28-1202)

NEVADA

Manufacture or importation of dangerous weapon; possession or use of silencer or dangerous weapon; carrying concealed weapon, without permit; issuance of permit; penalties. 1. It is unlawful for any person within this state to: (a) Manufacture or cause to be manufactured, or import into the state, or keep, offer or expose for sale, or give, lend or possess any knife which is made an integral part of a belt buckle or any instrument or weapon of the kind commonly known as a switchblade knife, blackjack, slung shot, billy, sand-club, sandbag or metal knuckles; or (b) carry concealed upon his person any: (1) Explosive substance, other than ammunition or any components thereof; (2) Dirk, dagger or dangerous knife; (3) Pistol, revolver or other firearm, or other dangerous or deadly weapon; or (4) Knife which is made an integral part of a belt buckle. 2. It is unlawful for any person to possess or use a: (a) Nunchaku or trefoil with the intent to inflict harm upon the person of another; or (b) Machine gun or a silencer... 5. As used in this section:... (b) "Nunchaku" means an instrument consisting of two or more sticks, clubs, bars or rods connected by a rope, cord, wire or chains used as a weapon in forms of Oriental combat... (e) "Trefoil" means an instrument consisting of a metal plate having three or more radiating points with sharp edges designed in the shape of a star, cross or other geometric figure and used as a weapon for throwing. (202.350)

NEW HAMPSHIRE

...V. "Deadly weapon" means any firearm, knife or other substance or thing which, in the manner it is used, intended to be used, or threatened to be used, is known to be capable of producing death or serious bodily injury. VI. "Serious bodily injury" means any harm to the body which causes severe, permanent or protracted loss or impairment to the health or the function of any part of the body. (625:11)

NEW JERSEY

...r. "Weapon" means anything readily capable of lethal use or of inflicting serious bodily injury. The term includes, but is not limited to, all (1) firearms, even though not loaded or lacking a clip or another component to render them immediately operable; (2) components which can be readily assembled into a weapon; (3) gravity knives, switchblade knives, daggers, dirks, stilettos, or other dangerous knives, billies, blackjacks, bludgeons, metal knuckles, sandclubs, slingshots, cesti or similar leather bands studded with metal fillings or razor blades imbedded in wood; and (4) stun guns; and any weapon or other device which projects, releases, or emits tear gas or any other substance intended to produce temporary physical discomfort or permanent injury through being vaporized or otherwise dispensed in the air... (2C:39-1)

NEW MEXICO

"Carrying a deadly weapon." "Carrying a deadly weapon" means being armed with a deadly weapon by having it on the person, or in close proximity thereto, so that the weapon is readily accessible for use. (30-7-1)

Unlawful carrying of a deadly weapon. A. Unlawful carrying of a deadly weapon consists of carrying a concealed loaded firearm or any other type of deadly weapon anywhere, except in the following cases: (1) in the person's residence or on real property belonging to him as owner, lessee, tenant or licensee; (2) in a private automobile or other private means of conveyance, for lawful protection of the person's or another's person or property; (3) by a peace officer in accordance with the policies of his law enforcement agency who is certified pursuant to the Law Enforcement Training Act (29-7-1 to 29-7-11 NMSA); or (4) by a peace officer in accordance with the policies of his law enforcement agency who is employed on a temporary basis by that agency and who has successfully completed a course of firearm instruction prescribed by New Mexico law enforcement academy or provided by a certified firearms instructor who is employed on a permanent basis by a law enforcement agency. B. Nothing in this section shall be construed to prevent the carrying of any loaded firearm. C. Whoever commits unlawful carrying of a deadly weapon is guilty of a petty misdemeanor. (30-7-2)

Unlawful possession of switchblades. Unlawful possession of switchblades consists of any person, either manufacturing, causing to be manufactured, possessing, displaying, offering, selling, lending, giving away or purchasing any knife which has a blade which opens automatically by hand pressure applied to a button, spring or other device in the handle of the knife, or any knife having a blade which opens or falls or is ejected into position by the force of gravity or by any outward centrifugal thrust or movement. Whoever commits unlawful possession of switchblades is guilty of a petty misdemeanor. (30-7-8)

Possession of explosives or explosive or incendiary device. A. Possession of explosives or explosive or incendiary device consists of possessing, manufacturing or transporting any explosive or any explosive or incendiary device, including any combination of parts from which such device may be made... (30-7-19)

NEW YORK

Definitions. As defined in the Penal Law, the term "crime" includes a misdemeanor or felony. "Physical injury" is defined to mean impairment of physical condition or sustain pain. "Serious physical injury" means physical injury which creates a substantial risk of death or which causes death or serious and protracted disfigurement, protracted impairment of health or protracted loss or impairment of function of any bodily organ. As defined in the Penal Law, the term "deadly physical force" means physical force which, under the circumstances in which it is used is readily capable of causing death or other serious physical injury. The term "deadly weapon" is declared to mean any loaded weapon from which a shot, readily capable of producing death or other serious physical injury, may be discharged, or a switchblade knife, gravity knife, dagger, billy, blackjack, or metal knuckles... (S.8)

Criminal possession of weapon—fourth degree. Although the possession of certain weapons may be licensed, and although there are various statutory exceptions to the general prohibitions against possession of certain weapons, as discussed in this and the sections immediately following, the Penal Law declares the mere possession of certain weapons to be criminal or unlawful. A person is guilty of criminal possession of a weapon in the fourth degree when: (1) he possesses any firearm, electronic dart gun, gravity knife, switchblade knife, cane sword, billy, blackjack, bludgeon, metal knuckles, chuka stick, sandbag, sandclub, or slungshot, or (2) he possesses any dagger, dangerous knife, dirk, razor, stiletto, imitation pistol, shuriken, or "Kung Fu Star," which is a disc-like object with sharpened points on its circumference and is designed for use primarily as a weapon to be thrown, or any other dangerous or deadly instrument or weapon with intent to use it unlawfully against another... (S.1581)

NORTH CAROLINA

Carrying concealed weapons. (a) It shall be unlawful for any person, except when on his own premises, willfully and intentionally to carry concealed about his person any bowie knife, dirk, dagger, slung shot, loaded cane, metallic knuckles, razor, shuriken, stun gun, pistol, gun or other deadly weapon of like kind. This section does not apply to an ordinary pocketknife carried in a closed position. As used in this section, "ordinary pocket knife" means a small knife, designed for carrying in a pocket or purse, which has its cutting edge and point entirely enclosed by its handle, and that may not be opened by a throwing, explosive or spring action... (14-269)

NORTH DAKOTA

General definitions. As used in this title, unless the context otherwise requires: 1. "Dangerous weapon" includes any switchblade or gravity knife, machete, scimitar, stiletto, sword, dagger, or knife with a blade of five inches (12.7 centimeters) or more; any throwing star, nunchaku, or other martial arts weapon; any billy, blackjack, sap, bludgeon, cudgel, metal knuckles, or sand club; any slungshot; any bow and arrow, crossbow, or spear; any stun gun; any weapon that will expel, or is readily capable of expelling, a projectile by the action

138

of a spring, compressed air, or compressed gas including any such weapon, loaded or unloaded, commonly referred to as a BB gun, air rifle, or C02 gun; and any projector of a bomb or any object containing or capable of producing and emitting any noxious liquid gas, or substance... (62.1-01-01)

OHIO

Definitions. The Criminal Code, as used in those sections of such Code dealing with weapons control, defines the following terms: "deadly weapon;" "firearm;" "handgun;" "semiautomatic firearm;" "automatic firearm;" "sawed-off firearm;" "zip-gun;" "explosive device;" "incendiary device;" and "dangerous ordinance." (2382)

OKLAHOMA

Carrying weapons—Exceptions. It shall be unlawful for any person to carry upon or about his person, or in his portfolio or purse, any pistol, revolver, dagger, bowie knife, dirk knife, switchblade knife, spring-type knife, sword cane, knife having a blade which opens automatically by hand pressure applied to a button, spring, or other device in the handle of the knife, blackjack, loaded cane, billy, hand chain, metal knuckles, or any other offensive weapon, except as in this article provided. Provided further, that this section shall not prohibit the proper use of guns and knives for hunting, fishing or recreational purposes... (1272)

OREGON

...(1) "Dangerous weapon" means any instrument, article or substance which under the circumstances in which it is used, attempted to be used or threatened to be used, is readily capable of causing death or serious physical injury. (2) "Deadly weapon" means any instrument, article or substance specifically designed for and presently capable of causing death or serious physical injury... (161.015)

PENNSYLVANIA

Definitions. "Deadly weapon." Any firearm, whether loaded or unloaded, or any device designed as a weapon and capable of producing death or serious bodily injury, or any other device or instrumentality which, in the manner in which it is used or intended to be used, is calculated or likely to produce death or serious bodily injury... (2301)

RHODE ISLAND

Weapons other than firearms prohibited.—No person shall carry or possess or attempt to use against another, any instrument or weapon of the kind commonly known as a blackjack, slingshot, billy, sandclub, sandbag, metal knuckles, bludgeon, or the so called "Kung-Fu" weapons, nor shall any person, with intent to use the same unlawfully against another, carry or possess a dagger, dirk, stiletto, sword-in-cane, bowie knife, or other similar weapon designed to cut and stab another, nor shall any person wear or carry concealed upon his person, any of the aforesaid instruments or weapons, or any razor, or knife of any description having having a blade of more than three (3) inches in length measuring from the end of the handle where the blade is attached to the end of said blade, or other weapon of like kind or description... (11-47-42)

SOUTH CAROLINA

Definition of "weapon"; confiscation and disposition of weapons used in commission or in furtherance of crime. (1) Except for the provisions relating to rifles and shotguns in 16-23-460 as used in this chapter, "weapon" means firearm (rifle, shotgun, pistol, or similar device that propels a projectile through the energy of an explosive), a knife with a blade over two inches long, a blackjack, a metal pipe or pole, or any other type of device or object which may be used to inflict bodily injury or death... (16-23-405)

SOUTH DAKOTA

...(6) "Concealed," any firearm that is totally hidden from view. If any part of the firearm is capable of being seen, it is not concealed;... (l0) "Dangerous weapon" or "deadly weapon," any firearm, knife or device, instrument, material or substance, whether animate or inanimate, which is calculated or designed to inflict death or serious bodily harm, or by the manner in which it is used or is likely to inflict death or serious bodily harm... (22-1-2)

TENNESSEE

Prohibited weapons.—(a) A person commits an offense who intentionally or knowingly possesses, manufactures, transports, repairs or sells: (1) An explosive or an explosive weapon; (2) A device principally designed, made or adapted for delivering or shooting an explosive weapon; (3) A machine gun; (4) A short-barrel rifle or shotgun; (5) A firearm silencer; (6) A switchblade knife or knuckles; or (7) Any other implement for infliction of serious bodily injury or death which has no common lawful purpose... (39-17-1302)

TEXAS

What constitutes a "deadly weapon." A deadly weapon is defined by the Penal Code as a firearm or anything manifestly designed, made, or adapted for the purpose of inflicting death or serious bodily injury, or anything that in the manner of its use or intended use is capable of causing death or serious bodily injury. Neither the degree of injury nor the fact of its infliction necessarily determines the character of a weapon as deadly. Thus, although a wound inflicted on the victim is a factor in determining whether the weapon used was a deadly weapon, the infliction of a wound is not necessary in order to determine that the weapon used was a deadly weapon. (421)

UTAH

Uniform law—Definitions. (c) "Dangerous weapon" means any item that in the manner of its use or intended use is capable of causing death or serious bodily injury. In construing whether an item, object, or thing not commonly known as a dangerous weapon is a dangerous weapon, the character of the instrument, object, or thing; the character of the wound produced, if any; and the manner in which the instrument, object, or thing was used are determinative... (76-10-501)

VERMONT

Slung shot, blackjack, brass knuckles—Use or possession. A person who uses a slung shot, blackjack, brass knuckles or similar weapon against another person, or attempts so to do, or who possesses a slung shot, blackjack, brass knuckles, or similar weapon, with intent so to use it, shall be imprisoned not more than five years or fined not more than $1,000 or both. The provisions of this section do not apply to a law enforcement office as to the possession and use of a blackjack, billy club or night stick. (4001)

VIRGINIA

Carrying concealed weapons; when lawful to carry.—A. If any person carries about his person, hidden from common observation, (i) any pistol, revolver, or other weapon designed or intended to propel a missile of any kind, or (ii) any dirk, bowie knife, switchblade knife, ballistic knife, razor, slingshot, spring stick, metal knucks, blackjack, or (iii) any flailing instrument consisting of two or more rigid parts connected in such a manner as to allow them to swing freely, which may be known as a nunchaka, nun chuck, nunchaku, shuriken, or fighting chain, or (iv) any disc of whatever configuration, having at least two points or pointed blades which is designed to be thrown or propelled and which may be known as a throwing star or oriental dart, or (v) any weapon of like kind as those enumerated in this subsection... (18-2-308)

WASHINGTON

Dangerous weapons—Evidence. Every person who shall manufacture, sell or dispose of or have in his possession any instrument or weapon of the kind usually known as slung shot, sand club, or metal knuckles, or spring blade knife, or any knife the blade of which is automatically released by a spring mechanism or other mechanical device, or any knife having a blade which opens, or falls, or is ejected into position by the force of gravity, or by an outward, downward, or centrifugal thrust or movement; who shall furtively carry with intent to conceal any dagger, dirk, pistol, or other dangerous weapon; or who shall use any contrivance or device for suppressing the noise of any firearm, shall be guilty of a gross misdemeanor. (9.41.250)

Weapons apparently capable of producing bodily harm, carrying, exhibiting, displaying or drawing unlawful—penalty—Exceptions. (1) It shall be unlawful for anyone to carry, exhibit, display or draw any firearm, dagger, sword, knife or other cutting or stabbing instrument, club, or any other weapon apparently capable of producing bodily harm, in a manner, under circumstances, and at a time and place that either manifests an intent to intimidate another or that warrants alarm for the safety of other persons... (9.41.270)

Students carrying dangerous weapons on school premises—Penalty—Exceptions. (1) It is unlawful for an elementary or secondary school student under the age of twenty-one knowingly to carry onto public or private elementary or secondary school premises: (a) Any firearm; or (b) Any dangerous weapon as defined in RCW 9.41.250; or (c) Any device commonly known as "nun-chu-ka sticks," consisting of two or more lengths of wood, metal, plastic, or similar substance connected with wire, rope, or other means; or (d) Any device, commonly known as "throwing stars," which are multi-pointed, metal objects designed to embed upon impact from any aspect... (9.41.280)

WEST VIRGINIA

As used in this article, unless the context otherwise requires: (1) "Blackjack" means a short bludgeon consisting, at the striking end, of an encased piece of lead or some other heavy substance and, at the handle end, a strap or springy shaft which increases the force of impact when a person or object is struck. The term "blackjack" shall include, but not be limited to, a billy, billy club, sand club, sandbag, or slapjack. (2) "Gravity knife" means any knife that has a blade released from the handle by the force of gravity or the application of centrifugal force, and when so released is locked in place by means of a button, spring, lever, or other locking or catching device. (3) "Knife" means an instrument, intended to be used or readily adaptable to be used as a weapon, consisting of a sharp-edged or sharp-pointed blade, usually made of steel, attached to a handle, which is capable of inflicting cutting, stabbing or tearing wounds. The term "knife" shall include, but not be limited to, any dagger, dirk, poniard or stiletto with a blade over three and one-half inches in length, any switchblade knife or gravity knife, and any other instrument capable of inflicting cutting, stabbing, or tearing wounds. A pocketknife with a blade three and one-half inches or less in length, a hunting or fishing knife carried for hunting, fishing, sports or other recreational uses, or a knife designed for use as a tool or household implement shall not be included within the term "knife" as defined herein, unless such knife is knowingly used or intended to be used to produce serious bodily injury or death. (4) "Switchblade knife" means any knife having a spring-operated blade which opens automatically upon pressure being applied to a button, catch or other releasing device in its handle. (5) "Nunchuka" means a flailing instrument consisting of two or more rigid parts, connected by a chain, cable, rope or other non-rigid, flexible or springy material, constructed in such a manner as to allow the rigid parts to swing freely, so that one rigid part may be used as the striking end. (6) "Metallic or false knuckles" means a set of finger rings attached to a transverse piece, to be worn over the front of the hand for use as a weapon, and constructed in such a manner that, when striking another person with the fist or closed hand, considerable physical damage may be inflicted upon the person struck. The term "metallic or false knuckles" shall include any such instrument, without reference to the metal or other substance or substances from which the metallic or false knuckles are made. (7) "Pistol" means a short firearm having a chamber which is integral with the barrel, designed to be aimed and fired by the use of a single hand. (8) "Revolver" means a short firearm having a cylinder of several chambers that are brought successively into line with the barrel to be discharged, designed to be aimed and fired by the use of a single hand. (9) "Deadly weapon" means an instrument which is designed to be used to produce serious bodily injury or death, or is readily adaptable to such use. The term "deadly weapon" shall include, but not be limited to, the instruments defined in subdivisions (1) through (8) of this section, or other deadly weapons of like kind or character which may be easily concealed on or about the person... (61-7-2)

WISCONSIN

...(10) "Dangerous weapon" means any firearm, whether loaded or unloaded, any device designed as a weapon capable of producing death or great bodily harm, any electrical weapon, as defined in s. 941.295(4); or any other device or instrumentality which, in the manner it is used or intended to be used, is calculated or likely to produce death or great bodily harm... (939.22)

WYOMING

Definitions. (iv) "Deadly weapon" means but is not limited to a firearm, explosive or incendiary material, motorized vehicle, an animal or other device, instrument, material or substance, which in the manner it is used or is intended to be used is reasonably capable of producing death or serious bodily injury... (6-1-104)

DISTRICT OF COLUMBIA

Possession of certain dangerous weapons prohibited; exceptions. (a) No person shall within the District of Columbia possess any machine gun, sawed-off shotgun, or any instrument or weapon of the kind commonly known as a blackjack, slungshot, sand club, sandbag, switchblade knife, or metal knuckles, nor any instrument, attachment, or appliance for causing the firing of any firearm to be silent or intended to lessen or muffle the noise of the firing of any firearms... (22-3214)

GUAM

Manufacture, sale, carrying, etc., certain dangerous weapons, prohibited. (a) Every person who within the Territory of Guam manufactures, or causes to be manufactured, or who imports into the Territory of Guam, or who keeps for sale, or offers or exposes for sale, or who gives, lends or possesses any instrument or weapon of the kind commonly known as a blackjack, slung shot, billy, sandclub, sandbag, metal knuckles, or any knife the blade of which opens by means of a spring or other automatic or semiautomatic device, commonly known as a switch knife, or any knife having a blade which opens or falls or is ejected into position by the force of gravity, or by an outward, downward or centrifugal thrust or movement, commonly known as a gravity knife, shall be guilty of a misdemeanor and upon conviction thereof shall be punishable by a fine of not more than $500 or by imprisonment for not more than one year, or both. (b) Every person who carries openly or concealed upon his person any explosive substance, other than fixed ammunition, or any dirk, dagger, switch or gravity knife as defined in (a) hereof, or any knife having a blade more than three inches in length, shall be guilty of a felony and upon conviction thereof shall be subject to confinement of not less than one (1) year, nor more than five years, and in no case may probation or suspension of sentence be granted and in addition may be subjected to a fine of not to exceed $1,000. It shall be a defense to a charge of carrying a knife having a blade more than three inches in length under this subsection to show that such knife was reasonably required in the pursuit of a trade or profession or for ordinary household, hunting, or fishing purposes; and it shall be a defense to a charge of carrying any explosive substance, other than fixed ammunition, to show compliance with pertinent licensing statutes and regulation. (c) Nothing in this Section shall prohibit any peace officer or law enforcement officer from carrying any wooden club, baton, or any equipment authorized by the properly constituted authorities for the enforcement of law or regulations. (d) For the purposes of this Section a machete or a bolo having a blade of at least twelve (12) inches in length, and only one sharpened edge, shall not be considered a knife. (642)

PUERTO RICO

Definitions. For the purpose of this chapter, the phrases and terms hereinafter listed shall have the following meaning and definition:... (q) A "ninja star" is a flat metal instrument with many sharp edges that can be shaped like a star, commonly used in the oriental martial arts, which is thrown or hurled. (454)

VIRGIN ISLANDS

Carrying or using dangerous weapons. (a) Whoever—(1) has, possesses, bears, transports, carries or has under his proximate control any instrument or weapon of the kind commonly known as a blackjack, billy, sandclub, metal knuckles, bludgeon, switchblade knife or gravity knife or electric weapon or device; or (2) with intent to use the same unlawfully against another, has, possesses, bears, transports, carries or has under his proximate control, a dagger, dirk, dangerous knife, razor, stiletto, or any other dangerous or deadly weapon shall—(A) be fined not more than $1,000 or imprisoned not more than two (2) years, or both; or (B) if he has previously been convicted of a felony, or has, possesses, bears, transports, carries or has under his proximate control, any such weapon during the commission or attempted commission of a crime of violence (as defined in section 2253(d)(1) hereof) shall be fined not more than $2,000 or imprisoned not more than five (5) years, or both, which penalty shall be in addition to the penalty provided for the commission of, or attempt to commit, the crime of violence. (b) For purposes of subsection (a) of this section, the term "switchblade knife" means any knife which has a blade which opens automatically by hand pressure applied to a button, spring, or other device in the handle of the knife; and the term "gravity knife" means any knife which has a blade which is released from the handle or sheath thereof by the force of gravity or the application of centrifugal force which, when released, is locked in place by means of a button, spring, lever or other device; and the term "electrical weapon or device" means any device which, through the application or use of electric current, including battery-operated devices, is designed, redesigned, used, or intended to be used for offensive or defensive purposes, the destruction of life, or the infliction of injury... (2251)

Judicial Interpretation of State Statutes
Pertaining to Martial Arts Weapons

It is axiomatic that state legislatures write the laws and state courts interpret those laws. No lawyer worth his or her salt would end research by just reading the relevant statute. That begins, not ends, the inquiry.

While legislatures paint the broad strokes, courts step in with the fine details, applying the statutory provisions to real-world flesh-and-blood instances, cases if you please. It should be noted that the cases which follow—and for that matter all the cases referred to in this text—are *appellate* cases. This means that in each and every case we are dealing with at least one court removed from the trial stage. If no appeal was taken (which occurs in most instances), there will be no recorded opinion and hence the matter will be "unreported." So throughout this book we are dealing with the opinion of a panel of judges who are reviewing what went on at trial and are deciding if all's jake.

American courts have discussed cases dealing with *nunchaku*, samurai swords, manrikigusari, *sai*, shuriken, *balisong* knives, and even "ninja claws."

Far and away, the nunchaku is the martial arts weapon most often discussed in American case law. Perhaps this is due to the popularization of nunchaku by Bruce Lee. It may be impossible to enter any martial arts store in America without being confronted with a shelf or two dedicated to nunchaku—steel, wooden, rubber and plastic—connected by chain, rope, plastic cord, etc. It has become the martial artist's weapon of choice, and understandably so. Unfortunately, it has also become the wanna-be martial artist's weapon of choice. As the alert reader will note, most of the people who run afoul of the law in the cases that follow were questionable martial artists, and even that's a stretch. What we deal with here, in the main, are those of the criminal persuasion who haplessly get caught with nunchaku in their possession.

Be prepared for some advanced bastardization of "nunchaku." My favorite is Numb Chucks. Is this a bunch of guys named Charlie who had a few too many drinks?

Most readers are familiar with the rise of the lowly "grain thresher" as a deadly weapon. When Japan conquered the island of Okinawa, a weapons ban was issued that would thrill a Democrat. It was "gun control" run amok. No weapons, particularly swords. No weapons at all, period.

So the Okinawan farmer grinned, picked up his rice thresher, and turned it into a spinning club that could explode a coconut and a "nutcracker" that could snap bones. Hence: the nunchaku. And American courts have had a great deal to say about this rice thresher, more so by far than all the sai, manrikigusari, samurai swords, shuriken and ninja claws put together.

The Dreaded Nunchaku

Of the almost 50 cases in this section, more than two-thirds deal with nunchaku—twice as many cases as all the other martial arts weapons *combined!*

Nunchaku can explode coconuts like grenades, crack bones and strangle. It is considered a deadly weapon by almost all jurisdictions. The following is what the courts have said.

The case of *In Re S.P.* gives a better than usual discussion. Here, police approached the defendant in downtown Washington, "in the midst of (a) crowd swinging and twirling around his body what the officers recognized as nunchaku..." He was arrested and convicted under D.C. law for "carrying a deadly or dangerous weapon, nunchaku sticks, capable of being concealed on or about his person..."

The appellate court upheld the conviction and in the course of its opinion stated:

At trial, Officer Michael Vitug was qualified by the court as an expert in the martial arts and related weaponry... Vitug stated that the nunchaku is used by martial arts experts at sports events in individual demonstrations of dexterity and fitness, but is not used in combative sports because of its capacity to cause great injury or death."

Vitug testified that the nunchaku derives its dangerous and potential lethal qualities from its design and construction. He noted that the nunchaku can be handled with silence and great speed and that when swung, it becomes a potent offensive weapon... Vitug identified the instrument appellant carried as a speedchaku, a variant of the nunchaku, and noted that it was available at many local stores. The speedchaku contains 'swivels...(with) ballbearings' making it faster when swung. It is also heavier than the usual nunchaku...and is considerably more dangerous...'

Taking all this into account, the court upheld the appellant's conviction and noted:

We recognize the nunchaku has socially acceptable uses within the context of martial arts and for the purpose of developing physical dexterity and coordination. Nevertheless, because of the inherent character of the nunchaku as an offensive weapon and its ready commericial availability...we must be cognizant also of its potential for illicit use.

Is The Nunchaku A Club?

Unlike the District of Columbia, many jurisdictions do not mention nunchaku *per se* in their deadly weapons statutes. In such cases, jurists must decide whether the nunchaku is a "club" or a "bludgeon" and thus covered by implication. The courts are split.

The case of *Tatom v. State* is both instructive and representative. Here, two brothers were speeding in their van, and were pulled over by the police. In the words of the court, "As the officers approached they observed a pair of 'nun-chucks' between the seats on the engine cover.

A nun-chuck [sic] consists of two sticks which are connected by chain or cord. They are used by those trained in the discipline of karate. The brothers were arrested for unlawfully carrying a weapon."

The appellant contended that a nun-chuck was not a club as defined in the statute, which defined club as:

'Club' means an instrument that is specifically designed, made, or adapted for the purpose of inflicting serious bodily injury or death by striking a person with the instrument, and includes but is not limited to the following: (A) blackjack; (B) nightstick; (C) mace; (D) tomahawk... A person commits an offense if he intentionally, knowingly or recklessly carries on or about his person a club.

The court upheld the trial court's finding that nunchaku were clubs under the meaning of the statute.

In the nasty case of *Toledo v. Texas,* the Texas court referred to the above case to find that forcing a mother and daughter to masturbate with nunchaku was "rape with a deadly weapon."

Other courts have disagreed and have declared that nunchaku were not "bludgeons" (weighted clubs). Two of these cases come from Illinois. First is the case of *People v. Tate.* Here, the defendant/appellant was a *karateka,* and he was nabbed by the police on his way home from karate class, carrying nunchaku. The trial court held that the martial arts weapons were "bludgeons" and the appellate court disagreed, overturning the conviction. The court held that the nunchaku were part of a legitimate sport and that "a bludgeon is a stick with one end loaded or thicker or heavier than the other end. There is nothing in the record to indicate that one end of the instant karate sticks was loaded or thicker or heavier than the other end and we therefore cannot conclude that the instant karate sticks falls within the definition of a bludgeon."

Two years later, the Third District of the Appellate Court of Illinois found similarly in *City of Pekin v. Shindledecker.* The appellate court held that a set of "num-chucks" [sic] protruded from underneath the driver's seat of the defendant's car and were observed when he was stopped for a routine traffic violation (inoperable taillights). Since these "num-chucks" were not specifically proscribed by statute and were not "bludgeons," there was no basis for the initial arrest. Thus, the marijuana the police found was suppressed and the defendant/appellant walked.

Lastly, the Michigan Court of Appeals found similarly in *People v. Malik.* The court not only found nunchaku not to be a bludgeon, or weighted club, but also found that "where the legislature lists items in a statute, it is the general rule that express mention of one thing implies the exclusion of other similar things *(expressio unius est exclusio alterius)."* That is my favorite legal phrase, hands down. It rolls off the tongue.

Is The Nunchaku A "Deadly" Weapon?

It seems obvious to we martial artists that the nunchaku is a deadly weapon. Anyone who knows the basics of *shime-waza* (the strangulation techniques of judo and *jujitsu*) can see that. And in addition to generating enough power to explode a coconut on impact, the dreaded nunchaku is a garrote from hell.

However, since if you had two lawyers in a room you'd have three opinions, and since judges are trained attorneys...you have a difference of view on this subject.

The question of whether an item is a deadly weapon/dangerous weapon is critically important because in many states, like my home state—the Commonwealth of Kentucky—concealing a *deadly weapon* is a felony (unless you have a permit).

You can walk down the street with six-guns prominently displayed on your hips (this still happens in Hazard and bloody Harlan), and you're OK (at least you haven't offended Kentucky's "concealed deadly weapons statute"). But let the constabulary catch you with a shuriken or nunchaku in your pocket and you've got trouble in the Bluegrass State.

Further, the question of "concealment" aside, some states ban the carrying of "deadly" or "dangerous" weapons—concealed or not—period.

So the question of whether nunchaku are "deadly" or "dangerous" weapons is important to martial artists who practice with weapons.

The following courts have concluded that nunchaku are "deadly" or "dangerous" weapons—with all the attendant legal consequences:

* *State v. Mitchell:* "The device (nunchaku) survives today only as a weapon." (An excellent discussion followed as to what you can do to harm and kill with nunchaku.)

* *R.V. v. State:* "Unlike other common objects which may be deadly only because of their use or threatened use, the sole modern use of a nunchaku is to cause great bodily harm... The instrument's historical origin (as a farm tool) does not help persuade us that it has constructive social utility on the streets of urban Miami."

* *State v. Tucker:* "Given the construction of the statute we have applied, nunchaku sticks fit within the prohibition of the general terms. They are primarily designed and intended for use in combat with the purpose of causing injury or death. Indeed, the legislature has recognized their character by including them specifically as a dangerous or deadly weapon regulated by ORS 166.220."

* *People v. White:* "It is for you (the jury) to determine from all of the facts and circumstances disclosed by the evidence *whether there was a dangerous weapon in question* here or whatever was used, the Nunchuck sticks [sic], if you believe there were such things, were, indeed, were a dangerous weapon." The appellate court upheld the jury's finding that the nunchaku, used to effectuate rape, was a dangerous weapon.

* *State v. Lupien:* "There can be no doubt that a weapon such as numchuks [sic], capable of shattering a clavicle in one quick strike, constitutes a deadly weapon for purposes of 13 V.S.A. sec. 1024(a)(2)."

* *State v. Mullen:* "...(I)f the nunchuckas [sic] was used in such a fashion as described...it could be lethal."

* *In re Reed:* "It is unnecessary to decide whether the mere possession of nunchaku sticks is a violation of the statute, because in the present case, one of the arresting officers testified that Reed actually threatened them with the weapon..."

* *People v. Wethington:* "As the defendant notes, the courts of Illinois have twice held that numchucks [sic] or karate sticks are not *per se* deadly weapons *(City of Pekin v. Shindledecker* and *People v. Tate,* noted above). However, in both (those cases), the defendants were merely in possession of the instrument and were not charged with

using it as a weapon in an assault... The trial court concluded in the instant case that the defendant had used the karate sticks in such a manner as to make them a deadly weapon. We find no error in the trial court's decision."

Other courts have found nunchaku *not* to be a deadly/dangerous weapon. Here's what they've said:

* *State v. Maloney:* "There is nothing in the record before this court to indicate that the device (nunchaku) was designed or specifically adapted for use as a weapon... Instead, the evidence tends to indicate that the device was used only for lawful purposes."

* *Commonwealth v. Adams:* Defendant was arrested on his way to karate school for carrying nunchaku—claimed to be a "prohibited offensive weapon." The appellate court overturned the finding. "Nunchaku sticks, not surprisingly, are not specifically enumerated as examples of offensive weapons (like "blackjacks, daggers and metal knuckles"). We need only determine whether it could serve a common lawful purpose... (T)here is no doubt that the nunchaku can be used offensively, as can a golf club or a baseball bat, to inflict serious injury. However, a student or instructor of the martial arts would have occasion to use the nunchaku in the peaceful practice of karate exercises. The martial arts are practiced by many citizens of this Commonwealth as a sport and an exercise. To eliminate the use, possession and sale of items used in this sport simply because they could conceivably be used to inflict bodily injury is contrary to the express purposes of (the statute)." (but see the Keastead case, below)

* *Keastead v. Commonwealth of Pa. Bd. of Probation & Parole:* "(W)e concluded that the Board was not wrong in ruling nunchakus to be a weapon for purposes of parole violation."

* *State of Hawaii v. Muliufi:* "Today, nunchaku sticks are widely used in the martial arts to build up dexterity, timing, mind and body coordination and aids in developing a larger sphere of consciousness around an individual... Given the present day uses of nunchaku sticks, we cannot say that the sole purpose of this instrumentality is to inflict death or bodily injury... We believe that nunchaku sticks, as used in the martial arts, are socially acceptable and lawful behavior, especially

here in Hawaii, where the oriental culture and heritage play a very important role in society. As such, nunchaku sticks are not a per se deadly or dangerous weapon within the meaning of HRS sec. 134-51."

The Dreaded Nunchaku In The Courtroom

In 1979 I ran successfully for Jefferson County (Louisville) Commissioner. My campaign "handlers" assiduously avoided or played-down the fact that I taught judo and kung fu because it was too much like "kinky sex."

A similar problem is faced by the trial lawyer representing any martial artist, especially one who is up on a martial arts weapons charge. And there's no weapon worse than the dreaded nunchaku— that is, if you want to avoid inflaming the jury.

Four courts discuss this matter. First, the case of *Toledo v. State* is instructive. The accused and convicted rapist, on appeal, complained "of the admission into evidence of a "nunchakus" [sic] device not shown to have any connection with him or the rapes... We hold that the trial court did not abuse its discretion by admitting a 'nunchakus' for the limited purpose of demonstration."

In another rape case, *Toledo v. Texas,* the Texas court held similarly: "There was no error in admitting into evidence a weapon similar to the one used in the attack for evaluation by the jury. The testimony of the martial arts instructor was admissible to show that the nunchakus was used or intended to be used in such a way that it was capable of causing death or serious bodily injury."

Thirdly, in *State v. Beeman,* a murder case, the court held:

The nunchucks [sic] rendered more probable the inferences that defendant caused the choke marks on the victim's neck...and that he had knowledge of the martial arts consistent with the ability to administer a devastating blow to (the victim's) forehead. We find (the) trial court did not abuse its discretion when it balanced probative value against undue prejudice in favor of admitting the num chucks [sic] into evidence.

Finally, in the case of *People v. Olsen* the court went even further and not only permitted introduction of the nunchaku into evidence— it allowed for a full-fledged demonstration before the jury!

That was jake with the appellate court, which held:

We conclude that the demonstration conducted in the present case was proper. Numchucks [sic] are martial arts instruments, and most jurors are not likely to be familiar with their use in this fashion. Numchucks [sic] may be deadly or dangerous, depending upon the manner in which they are used, and there was a fact question to be determined by the jury. The demonstration in the present case was relevant to show how numchucks [sic] are designed and can be used and how they may have been used in the present case. There was evidence that defendant knew how to use numchucks [sic] and that he used them to inflict injuries on his victim. The demonstration was appropriate to aid the jury in determining whether the defendant was guilty of the offenses for which the use of a deadly or dangerous weapon was an element.

Enough on nunchaku—on to other martial arts weapons!

Other Martial Arts Weapons

After the dreaded nunchaku, other martial arts weapons pale in comparison and are seldom seen in a courtroom. What follows are some of the exceptions.

samurai swords

* *Cole v. State of Oklahoma:* Cop and samurai sword-wielding assailant scuffle.

* *Commonwealth v. Chandler:* Father stabs seven-year-old son in eye with "karate swords," blinding him.

* *State v. Sanders:* Vicious attack with samurai sword following accusations of burglary.

balisong knives

* *City of Columbus v. Dawson:* State proved balisong knife was designed specifically for use as a weapon.

* *People v. Mott:* Balisong or butterfly knife was not a "gravity knife" within statutory prohibition.

* *Taylor v. U.S.:* Customs seized balisong knives under the Switch Blade Knife Act; appellate court allowed importer to attempt to alter the knives to make them utilitarian and thus importable.

shuriken

* *Vaughn v. State:* Defendant's conviction for "intimidation while armed" upheld after defendant waved shurikens in a threatening way.

A *shuriken* would have to be almost this size to do any damage as a
"deadly weapon."

* *Albert v. State of Texas:* "Martial arts throwing star" found to be
an illegal knife under the statute.

* *Hayes v. State of Texas:* Ditto. In Texas, a shuriken is treated as an
illegal knife.

Ninja Claws, Sai and Manrikigusari

Rounding out the weapons of mayhem are those which are exotic:

* *McQueen v. State:* Ninja claw found to be "deadly weapon."

* *Masters v. State:* Constitution of United States does not grant
appellant right to carry swords (sai) upon his person in public.

* *Commonwealth v. Brown:* In this case, a robbery-murder, an
insurance agent was shot after being strangled with the manrikigusari.
The court found it admissible to demonstrate use of the martial arts
weapon at trial.

This is how the courts have exercised their power to interpret

However, according to most statutes, a shuriken, no matter its size,
is considered a "deadly weapon."

statutes and balance common law equities. When searching the law in
your state, *annotated statutes* (deadly/dangerous weapons statutes and
others) will list current, controlling judicial interpretations of the laws
on the books, and they must be consulted.

There is no substitute for the advice of legal counsel.

CHAPTER SIX

Martial Arts Sports Injuries: Assumption of Risk and the Effect of Consent

C onsent plays an important role in determining the liability for sports injuries. The general rule is that one can't recover damages caused by an act to which he consented. This rule also applies to those who willingly participate in sports or athletic contests. It's been explained as follows: A person who enters into a sport, game

Judo *randori,*   karate sparring.

To what extent do you or your opponent assume the risk of injury
in competition judo and karate?

or contest may be taken to have consented to physical contact consistent with the understood rules of the game. Consent in this context is often discussed in terms of "assumption of risk." The law has been summarized:

A voluntary participant in a lawful game or contest assumes the risks ordinarily incident thereto, and he is precluded from recovering from his opponent or other participants for injury or death resulting therefrom, since, under the maxim of volenti non fit injuria, one is not legally injured by an assault committed in a lawful game if he has consented to the game and the incident assault.

This doctrine precludes recovery for injury or death resulting from participation in sports. Of course, these dangers must be *obvious* to be assumed. Assumption of risk, however, doesn't automatically bar *all* recovery for *all* sports injuries. The doctrine is hedged with numerous qualifications. The sports participant assumes only those risks and dangers normally seen as within the scope of the sport in which he's participating. If intentional acts causing injuries go beyond ordinarily permissible behavior in the sport, there may be recovery for assault and battery. There also can be no assumption of risk unless the participant understands the risks and voluntarily consents to undertake them. This consent covers only the particular acts which the participant knows are likely to occur, or acts of a substantially similar nature. (A consent to a fistfight is *not* consent to having a finger bitten.) A sports participant doesn't assume the risk of injury resulting from negligence, although recovery may be barred under the doctrine of contributory negligence. Finally, although sports participants may assume the ordinary dangers of a violent game, they don't assume the risk of injury inflicted intentionally.

Boxing illustrates the consent of participants in a dangerous contact sport:

The consent is to the plaintiff's conduct, rather than to its consequences. If the plaintiff willingly engages in a boxing match, he does not of course consent to be killed, but he does consent to the defendant's striking at him, and hitting him if he can; and if death unexpectedly results, his consent to the act will defeat any action for the resulting invasion of his interests.

This is qualified to the extent, according to some precedent, that the blow is struck with "no greater force than is justifiable under the circumstances." Also, the person delivering the abuse must not be guilty of either recklessness or negligent conduct in striking the killing or crippling blow.

The Restatement of Torts discusses the relationship between consent to sports injuries and legal liability:

Taking part in a game manifests a willingness to submit to such bodily contacts or restriction of liberty as they are permitted by its rules or usages.

The Restatement also defines the differences in the intent of rules: Participating in such a game does not manifest consent to contacts which are prohibited by rules or usages of the game if such rules or usages are designed to protect the participants and not merely to secure the better playing of the game as a test of skill. This is true although the player knows that those with or against whom he is playing are habitual violators of such rules.

Illustrations and examples describing the scope of consent in contact sports speckle the Restatement. Here are a few of these illustrations and examples:

A, while tackling B, deliberately injures him. A is subject to liability to B, whether the tackle was or was not otherwise within the rules and usages of football.

A, a member of a football team, tackles B, an opposing player, while he, A, is offside. The tackle is made with no greater violence than would be permissible by the rules and usages of football were he "onside." A has not subjected B to a violence greater than, or different from, that permitted by the rules, although he is guilty of a breach of a rule. A is not liable to B.

A and B engage in a boxing match. A thereby consents to B's efforts to hit him, and to the blows which he receives in the course of the match in accordance with its rules.

...There is no doubt that the consent would prevent recovery (where...) having confidence in his ability as an artful dodger, A consents to let B try to hit him. B succeeds despite A's dodging.

The legal liability for sports injuries has been discussed in numerous courts. Two cases decided by state appellate courts in 1904 held that *accidents* occurring during friendly scuffling or wrestling matches don't provide grounds for legal recourse. In *Nicholls v. Colwell,* the Illinois Appeals Court reversed the trial court's pre-emptory instructions for the defendant where the defendant allegedly injured the plaintiff, an 18-year-old female and former student of the defendant's, during a "playful scuffle." In the course of its opinion, the Illinois Appeals Court noted:

An action for assault and battery does not lie where an injury is done by unavoidable accident in the course of a friendly wrestling match or other lawful athletic sport, if not dangerous.

A similar position was taken the same year in *Gibeline v. Smith* by the Missouri Appeals Court. The plaintiff and defendant were friends. The defendant saw the plaintiff each time he collected for a brewery at the saloon housing the plaintiff's lunch counter. The plaintiff and the defendant joked and scuffled frequently upon meeting. On the day the injury occurred, the plaintiff was pushed into a showcase during their routine scuffle. The plaintiff and defendant then drank together and parted company. Later, the plaintiff discovered that his ribs were broken from the impact with the showcase. The appeals court affirmed the verdict for the defendant, holding:

It is our opinion that if the parties to this controversy each voluntarily engaged in a friendly scuffle, and the defendant, without intending to do so, accidentally hurt the plaintiff, no action will lie.

To hold otherwise, reasoned the court, "would be to say that all untoward results from the play of men or boys in which they mutually engage would furnish a cause of action by the injured party." The court pointed to the "sanction which ages have given" to rough and dangerous athletic contests to support the view that scuffling of the type engaged in by the plaintiff and the defendant was not unlawful.

However, courts have held for liability in some instances where participation in a lawful sport resulted in injury. As the Kansas Supreme Court noted in its 1905 *McNeil v. Mullin* decision, "...an injury, even in sport, would be an assault if it went beyond what was admissible in sports of the sort, and was intentional." Accordingly, the Massachusetts Supreme Court in *Fitzgerald v. Cavin* affirmed a verdict for the plaintiff who had his testicles squeezed (a foul hold) by the defendant in what was supposed to be a "friendly wrestling match by mutual consent."

Sports and contest injuries occur frequently in the martial arts. These injuries occur during both regular class sessions and tournaments. The two martial arts with the greatest sport flavor, organization and number of participants are judo and karate.

Judo has been described as "practically fool-proof against serious injury." Nevertheless, the sport is "made-to-order" for less serious, but

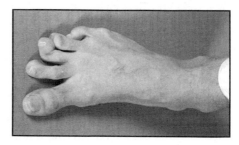

Judo is considered "the gentle way," and "practically fool-proof against serious injury," but less serious, nevertheless painful injuries do occur. Pictured are author Carl Brown's toes, mangled from years of judo practice.

nevertheless painful and vexing, injuries such as twisted elbows, sprained knees, bruised ankles and swollen toes. Although broken legs and arms are rare, broken toes and dislocated shoulders are common. Some *judoka* have suffered double hernias and knee injuries requiring major surgery.

Injuries rarely occur at judo tournaments because all judoka are taught surrender signals, and are taught how to fall. Pictured here are *judoka* "fighting for the choke."

Other judoka have had their heads split open, requiring stitches.

Those injuries are caused by the "lightning-fast throws and holds," joint locks, and strangles that make up the judo arsenal. These latter two categories of mayhem, joint locks and strangles, deserve particular mention. In a judo contest, one method of winning is to apply a joint lock to your opponent until he or she submits, the referee stops the match, or the bone breaks. Typically, the opponent knows when the technique has become inescapable, and submission readily follows. Another method to defeat your opponent is to apply a choke or strangulation technique, which cuts off his brain's oxygen supply. The match is won when the opponent either submits or is strangled into unconsciousness.

Despite the sanctioned use of dangerous armlocks and chokes, injuries rarely occur at judo tournaments. In the first place, all judoka are taught to slap or tap the mat, their opponent or their own thigh to signal that they're being injured. This command to cease is universally and quickly obeyed. Second, emphasis is typically placed on throws and pins, rather than armlocks and chokes, since these techniques are safer and account for most contest victories. (Judoka can also win contests with clean throws and solid pins.) And third, judoka are taught the proper way to fall to avoid injury while being thrown. A correctly executed fall can neutralize as much as 90 percent of the body's impact with the ground.

The use of surrender signals and the meticulous training in how to fall results in a lesser incidence of serious judo injuries. Although not all injuries are reported, it has been indicated through a variety of surveys taken at different times and different places that *serious* judo injuries are rare. Colonel Oliver E. Wood, U.S. Military attache at Tokyo near the turn of the century, reported to the War Department that out of the nearly 4,000 pupils who attended Dr. Kano's school of judo *(Kodokan)*, not one was permanently injured. Dr. Koiwai, a physician and fifth-degree black belt in judo, contends that "no death attributed directly to choking has been reported since the development of judo in 1882." According to a Marine judo instructor, over a four-year period during which 50,000 to 70,000 Marines received judo training at Parris Island, only one serious injury—a broken leg—occurred. In a survey conducted by the medical committee of the United States Judo Federation, it was reported that only 102 judo

Carl Brown and his assistant Richard Loeb demonstrate a *kansetsuwaza* armlock. When Brown (left) is attacked by a right overhand blow, he (1) catches it with his hands, encircling his attacker's wrist. Brown then (2) moves in a clockwise half turn, ultimately putting his left armpit against the attacker's right elbow. Pressure is exerted continuously until the attacker submits.

injuries occurred during a five-year period. "Fractures (34) were most commonly encountered, followed by shoulder injuries (27) and dislocations (16)." Judo, it seems, results in less injury to judoka than karate to *karateka.*

Karate is an entirely different story. Like judo, it's common to see many ankle, knee, back, neck and hand injuries, along with contusions, fractures, dislocations and sprains. Additionally, one sees more serious injuries in karate than in judo. When James T. King, Jr., MD, performed emergency surgery on Betti Bell (a karate student struck by her sparring partner), he found that the karate blow had destroyed 60 percent of her liver. She was lucky to survive. Others have not.

A Flagstaff, Arizona, general surgeon saved the life of a young man whose transverse colon had been torn by a karate kick. An Atlanta ophthalmologist treated a patient who suffered a detached retina from

Judoka are taught the proper way to fall to avoid injury when thrown. With this training, even high altitude falls from throws like *kata guruma* (shoulder wheel) are potentially safe.

the shock of a karate chop. Another physician recently reported to the *Medical Tribune* that a female patient's pancreas was severely damaged by a karate blow.

Countless other karateka have not survived the deadly blows received during karate instruction, training and competition. A young Californian died from kidney injuries the day following inept karate instruction. In 1974, a college student died after being struck in the spleen while practicing karate with a friend in Atlanta.

The occurrence of serious injuries and even death may be aggravated by the advent of full-contact karate tournaments. The Professional Karate Association has formed rules and procedures for full-contact karate competition. However, no single set of rules or procedures governs *all* karate tournaments. Some tournaments still require that punches and kicks be pulled to avoid dangerous injuries. Other tournaments permit contact, but require padding on the hands and feet, and sometimes even body armor. On the other extreme, some karate tournaments permit full-contact and forbid use of any padding or armor. One such tournament advertised with claims of "blood and proof of honor, no holds barred, no protective equipment, and all decisions by submission or knockout." It is generally agreed that kicks and chops delivered at these "professional contact karate tournaments" can easily maim. Enter the Ultimate Fighting Championship.

Liability for Injuries

Four settings for martial arts sports injuries will be analyzed: those injuries inflicted by a sparring partner or contest opponent, those received during "mutual combat," those caused by the negligence of the instructor, and those received during disciplining.

Injuries Inflicted by a Sparring Partner or Contest Opponent

When discussing contest injuries, a distinction should be drawn between judo and karate. Karate contest injuries occur more frequently and are usually more serious. Consequently, the standard for determining if *true* consent was given by the plaintiff should be higher for karateka than for judoka. The question is whether the karateka fully appreciated the risks related to competition. If not, grounds for legal action may exist.

A second consideration, particularly relevant to full-contact/no-padding karate matches, concerns exactly to what the plaintiff consented. Did the plaintiff consent to only a "contest" when he then engaged in a bloody battle? It runs contrary to some legal authority (and common sense) to allow the plaintiff to consent to negligent or intentional inflictions of injury. Given the existence and durability of boxing, there should be no legal problem with consenting to a full-

Punishing blows are common at martial arts tournaments. However, the
recipient of these blows is cushioned by foam rubber padding.

contact karate match or an Ultimate Fighting Championship (UFC).

A third consideration is whether a rule violated by either contestant was designed to protect the player or to better the playing of the game. Consent is no bar to a cause of legal action if the purpose of the violated rule is to protect the player. It may be a bar if the rule's purpose is merely to better the playing of the game. A rule prohibiting judo throws off the mat defies exclusive categorization, since the tournament sanction (the throw is awarded no points and the offender may be penalized) applies with equal force whether the victim of the bad throw lands on the border mat or in the bleachers. Also, a rule in some karate tournaments prohibiting throwing was put forth to not only minimize injuries, but to also encourage clean karate techniques and discourage brawling. In fact, many rules at judo and karate tournaments serve the dual purpose of protecting the contestants and encouraging the use of perfected techniques. The reasonable position seems to be that if the rule has as one of its purposes the protection of the martial artist, violation of such rule should allow legal action not barred by the injured party's initial consent.

A final consideration goes to the popular bare-knuckle, no-holds-barred karate bloodbaths. The continued occurrence of serious injuries at such publicity-generating extravaganzas, with most awarding prize money to the winners (or survivors), may result in these events being declared illegal (just as certain other types of spectator-geared combat have been declared illegal). Should this happen, contestants would not be engaged in a "lawful sport" and therefore in most jurisdictions would be allowed to recover for any injuries under the doctrine of "mutual combat." Contest will not prevent recovery.

Two appellate cases have dealt with injuries arising from a sparring partner. In *Kuehner v. Green,* Kuehner had been injured by a karate takedown maneuver executed by Green during a sparring session at Green's house. The case was tried before a jury which found both plaintiff and defendant fifty-percent negligent. Kuehner's damages totaled $55,000.

The jury was also given a special interrogatory (question):

Did the plaintiff (Kuehner) know of the existence of the danger complained of, realize and appreciate the possibility of injury as a result of such danger, and, having a reasonable opportunity to avoid it, voluntarily and deliberately expose himself to the danger complained of?

The jury responded to this question in the affirmative.

In turn, the trial court held that "sufficient evidence was presented to establish the defense of 'express assumption of risk.'" Therefore, the trial court rendered final judgment on behalf of Green, the defendant.

Most martial artists when they spar are well-protected from injury by the padding they wear.

On appeal, the district court agreed but certified to the Supreme Court of Florida the following question as "a matter of great public importance":

Does express assumption of risk absolutely bar a plaintiff's recovery where he engages in a contact sport with another participant who injures him without deliberate attempt to injure?

The Supreme Court of Florida found that the plaintiff in fact had expressly assumed the risk and that this barred his recovery.

In his concurring opinion, Judge Boyd put it in plain language:

In this case the plaintiff was injured when he fell as a result of a 'leg sweep.' Because the 'leg sweep' is a common karate maneuver, the defendant did not act in a reckless and therefore tortious manner. For this reason, I concur in the judgment...

In the case of *Scogin v. Century Fitness, Inc.*, a student who was injured while taking tae kwon do lessons brought action against a recreational center, alleging assault and battery and/or negligence. Scogin was injured while sparring with the instructor. He received a kick to his head, which fractured his cheekbone. The United States District Court for the Western District of Arkansas found on behalf of the recreational center. The United States Court of Appeals, Eighth Circuit, affirmed the decision. The questions on appeal were procedural in nature. The jury at trial apportioned that 55 percent of the fault lay with the injured student and 45 percent of the fault lay with the instructor. Under Arkansas law, this meant no recovery for the plaintiff.

Injuries Received During "Mutual Combat"

When fighters voluntarily and willingly square off, they're said to fight by "mutual combat." The majority of courts agree that consent to fight will not prevent recovery of injuries that might occur during the fight. The law has been expressed as follows:

In traditional sparring, each participant gives one another the consent to engage in a violent activity upon each other.

It is generally held that consent will not avail as a defense in a case of mutual combat, as such fighting is unlawful. Consequently, neither party to a fight, in which both fighters voluntarily engage, may defend on the ground that the fight resulted from a challenge or an acceptance thereof. Each person injured in a mutual combat may recover from the other all damages caused by the injuries received.

This position originated with an early English case, *Matthews v. Ollerton.* The case was decided when trespass was still a criminal and not a civil offense, and thus the state had an interest in the case. The modern justification for allowing damages even though consent was given is from a two-fold doctrine. It stresses the interest of the state in preventing the altercation, and recognizes the deterring effect that permitting damages should have on potential fighters. Negative opinions have been expressed regarding this policy:

The cases (allowing damages after mutual combat) have been roundly criticized on the grounds that no one should be rewarded with damages for his own voluntary participation in a wrong, particularly where, as is usually the case, he himself commits a crime; that the state is fully able to protect itself by a criminal prosecution; and that the parties, if they give any thought to the law at all, which is quite improbable, are quite as likely to be encouraged by the hope that if they get hurt they can still win in court.

A minority of states, supported by the Restatement, hold that consent to mutual combat defeats the civil action, except where the force

"At what point does sparring become mutual combat"? would be a question for the jury to decide.

employed during the conflict exceeds the consent. (Such as agreeing to a fistfight and having an opponent pull out a switchblade and stab you.) This assumes that the fighters, when they consented, were aware of the usual risks in fighting. As noted in the Restatement:

In the case of a fight or affray by mutual consent, each party gives consent to those blows from which he is unable to protect himself. But each consent to the other using such force as is reasonably necessary to defend himself against his opponent's attack.

The problem of mutual combat has been considered in numerous courts. The minority or restatement position barring recovery is reflected in *McAdams v. Windham,* a case decided by the Alabama Supreme Court in 1928. While engaged in a friendly bare-fisted boxing match, the defendant hit his opponent in the heart, killing him. The plaintiff, the deceased man's widow, filed a wrongful death action. The Alabama Supreme Court described the fight both as "mutual combat" and as "a mere sporting contest." In either event, the court affirmed the verdict for the defendant, noting that harm suffered after consenting to combat creates no cause of legal action.

The position, which says that consent to mutual combat *does not* defeat recovery for injuries received in said combat, is well-supported. In *Lewis v. Fountain,* a 1915 North Carolina case, the plaintiff visited the defendant's home to stop the defendant from threatening the plaintiff's sister. The testimony didn't clearly establish which party was the initial aggressor. The North Carolina Supreme Court considered the matter of "first aggressor" critical and held "when two men fight together, thereby creating an affray, each is guilty of assault and battery upon the other, and each can maintain an action therefore." The 1884 Wisconsin Supreme Court case of *Shay v. Thompson* held similarly where two farmers argued about the fence between their properties. The argument grew into a fight, during which the defendant gouged both eyes of the plaintiff. In affirming a $500 verdict for the plaintiff, the Wisconsin Supreme Court held "the fighting being unlawful, the consent of the plaintiff to fight is no bar to his action, and he is entitled to recover."

Apparently, the majority position allowing recovery of damages nevertheless allows evidence of consent to fight to lessen the damages recovered. The Rhode Island Supreme Court in its 1923 *Teolis v. Moscatelli* opinion referred to this "mitigation of damages." The Maine Supreme Court in its 1892 *Grotton v. Glidden* decision preferred to describe allowing evidence of consenting to fight as a measure to keep down the amount of the punitive damages, but not to reduce the actual damages.

Martial artists are generally trained to shun street confrontations. The mutual combat which martial artists prefer is a professional effort to develop and practice their skills. Called *randori* by judoka, or *kumite* by karateka, this combat takes place only within the *dojo* or tournament hall. A martial artist could be a mutual combatant in two settings: on the street and at tournaments (or in practice, but this is viewed differently—as was discussed previously). With respect to tournaments, it's likely that certain ones could be described as a series of "mutual combats." Some of the unrestrained full-contact matches have generated legal battles similar to hockey litigation.

If the description "mutual combat" applies to contact karate matches, the majority of courts would allow damages to injured participants. Courts agreeing with the Restatement position would bar recovery on the basis of consent, the same as if they viewed these matches as sports.

With respect to street fights, two legal issues are raised. The first issue involves the duty to warn. The Restatement requires only that the

Pictured is a demonstration of the judo technique *osotogari*. The *tori* (attacker) (1) begins with a right side normal holding position. The *uke's* (defender's) balance is broken (2-4) to his back left corner, then the tori's leg (with the toes pointed) is brought past the uke. Contact is made at the back of the uke's right knee and (5) the throw is accomplished. In *Klocek v. YMCA*, an instructor was unsuccessfully sued when a student was injured during the execution of this technique.

(Illustration 5 is shown from the left side in order to better illustrate the follow-through movement of the attacking leg.)

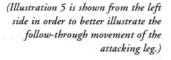

defendant warn of his intention to defend himself—and only if doing so won't hamper his defense. Nevertheless, as the previous analysis urged, the expert martial artist someday may be required by law to disclose his or her particular ability to ward off attack. If this duty is imposed in a self-defense situation (and even if it isn't), it certainly should be part of the requirement to validify consent to mutual combat. In order for the opposing party to consent properly and legally, it's imperative that the expert martial artist knows how "un-mutual" the combat might become.

The second issue concerns invasion of the plaintiff's interest by an act of a different character. If the martial artist fails to disclose his special skills and a fight occurs, the opposing party never consented to the punishment likely to be received by a trained fighter. This is similar to con-

senting to a boxing match and discovering that your opponent plans to load his gloves with buckshot. This being so, damages should be allowed under these circumstances, even in a Restatement jurisdiction. Identical analysis applies to the problem of "force exceeding consent."

Injuries Caused by the Negligence of the Instructor

Several appellate cases have dealt with injuries caused by instructor negligence. *Klocek v. YMCA of Metro Milwaukee* was decided by the Wisconsin Supreme Court in 1970. The plaintiff enrolled in a beginner's judo class offered by the YMCA. During the fifth week, the plaintiff was injured during a demonstration of *oso-togari* (a major outer reaping leg throw) by a substitute instructor, a first-degree black belt. The plaintiff charged the instructor with negligence, asserting that the substitute instructor was unqualified to teach judo.

In affirming the jury verdict for the defendant, the Wisconsin Supreme Court apparently considered three factors: the rank of the substitute instructor, the ability of the instructor to teach the technique which caused the plaintiff's injuries, and the traditional negligence factors. As to the first factor, (the rank of the substitute instructor), the court looked to the internal rank requirements of judo as taught in Wisconsin and found the substitute instructor's first-degree black belt rank qualified him to teach judo. The court stated:

The substitute instructor was a first-degree black belt, a rank or status certifying to and requiring weekly school attendance, knowledge as to lower ranks, understanding of judo training and instructional methods, and qualifying as able to conduct classes with the approval of the ranking yudansha or black belt instructor.

The second factor was the ability of the substitute instructor to teach the technique which gave rise to the plaintiff's injuries. Significantly, the court allowed expert testimony to establish the defendant's expertise. The highest-ranking black belt in Wisconsin testified that the substitute instructor taught the osotogari throw as well as any instructor he knew. Apparently accepting the truth of this testimony, the court found for the defendant.

As to the third and final factor (the traditional questions of negligence), again the court affirmed the jury's exoneration of the defendant:

Reviewing the record, we find no reason to quarrel with either judge or jury. As the jury found, there was credible evidence supporting a no-negligence finding. As the judge commented, it is difficult to find any evidence that would support a different conclusion.

In the case of *Wells v. Colorado College*, another judo instructor was accused of negligence. In response to a number of campus assaults, Colorado College arranged to offer its students a self-defense class, and hired two judo instructors from the Colorado Springs Police Department to conduct the class.

Coed Cheryl Wells was paired with a partner who was unable to throw her in a hip throw. One of the police instructors, to demonstrate the throw, tossed Ms. Wells on her back. Instead of hitting the mat, however, she hit the floor. The mats had separated and she landed partly between them. Due to her injures, Ms. Wells underwent surgery twice and missed one year of college. She received a $150,000 verdict against the college, and the United States Tenth Circuit Court of Appeals upheld the substantial verdict.

On appeal, the college contended that it was reversible error for the trial court to fail to instruct on "assumption of risk." The Tenth Circuit held:

In the case *Wells v. Colorado College*, the appellate court upheld a $150,000 verdict when a martial arts student was thrown on the floor during the execution of a technique when the mats separated. The court held that was one risk the student did not assume to take.

This is not a case involving participation in a sport which activity is commonly associated with the assumption of risk doctrine. Rather, the plaintiff was participating in a scheduled class and was doing it for a very practical reason. But even if we were to consider it as a sport, the evidence presented would still be deficient to support assumption of risk because it is not shown that the plaintiff anticipated an extraordinary hazard such as to which she was subjected. She had a right to expect that she would be thrown on the mat and not on the hardwood floor.

Another case contending instructor negligence is *Fantini v. Alexander.* The injured student was kicked in the head by a more advanced student during a demonstration "free fight." He claimed that the karate instructor acted negligently in having him participate in the match, since he received only 20 hours of instruction at the time of the kumite.

The trial court dismissed the case at the end of the plaintiff's proof "because plaintiff had failed to adduce testimony from an expert witness establishing a generally recognized standard of care from which defendant departed." The plaintiff's expert witness, a karate instructor, failed to establish any "generally accepted standard" regarding when a student should be ready to spar. The appellate court found that such matters were for the jury, not the judge, to determine (the trial court heard the expert testimony after excusing the jury). Further, the appellate court held that the plaintiff should have been allowed to put on additional evidence of his karate instructor's negligence which did not involve his conduct as a professional. The court reversed the dismissal and sent the case back for full trial.

A fourth appellate case claiming instructor negligence is *Brown v. Bridges.* Janet Lynn Hall filed suit against various defendants, claiming damages for injuries she suffered in a karate class. One of the defendants, Steve Stacy Brown, was the karate instructor at the time the injury occurred. Ms. Hall claimed that Mr. Brown "was not a qualified karate instructor, that he failed to properly demonstrate a particular karate maneuver referred to as a 'block and take-down' and further that this particular maneuver involved an unacceptable degree of risk for such inexperienced students as the plaintiff Hall." The court granted a third-party defendant's motion for leave to take a videotape deposition consisting of a demonstration by karate instructor Brown as to the manner and method of execution of the karate maneuvers in question. Brown appealed this motion to the appellate court, but it was denied. The appellate court found that the videotape deposition could be taken in light of the verbal inability to understand the techniques employed on the day of the accident. The appellate court also made mention of the stated need to submit the videotape to karate experts for evaluation of the competency of Brown's method of instruction.

The final case dealing with alleged instructor negligence is *Jackson v. Washington State Criminal Justice Training Commission.* The court set forth the facts as follows:

In September 1980, Mr. Jackson attended a Commission training session as a security officer with the Yakima County Sheriff's office. The curriculum included a physical force defensive tactics course instructed by Junki Yoshida, a karate expert who had developed police agency training programs in Oregon and other areas in the Northwest. Mr. Jackson was practicing a control technique with a partner when he sustained head and neck injuries rendering him unconscious for a period of time. The technique involved being taken to the floor by a fellow student and rendered immobile by a 'sleeper' hold which involved the application of pressure to the carotid artery. The actual execution of the maneuver involved grabbing a person's hair and turning his head slightly while pressing him to the floor in a prone position. The subject's neck was then positioned between the controlling partner's thigh and calf where pressure can be applied by a squatting motion. The final stage of the hold is designed to diminish blood supply to the brain, resulting in unconsciousness.

Mr. Jackson testified he did not remember whether they reached the final stage of the maneuver, i.e. whether any pressure was actually applied to his neck. Fellow students testified they were not in a position to observe what occurred between Mr. Jackson and Edward Maicke, his class partner, until after the injury. Mr. Maicke, however, testified the 'sleeper' was not applied and the injury in fact occurred during the 'take-down.' The students and Mr. Yoshida testified clear instructions were given that the sleeper should not be applied. Following the incident, Mr. Jackson was hospitalized and testified that he subsequently suffered loss of memory, headaches, depression and seizures.

Mr. Jackson's lawsuit resulted in a verdict for the defendants, and he appealed. Jackson claimed that the trial court erred in refusing a "*res ipsa loquitur* (the thing speaks for itself) instruction." The doctrine of res ipsa loquitur recognizes that an accident may happen "under circumstances that will allow the occurrence itself to circumstantially establish prima facie negligence on the part of the defendant, without further proof."

The appellate court decided that the elements necessary to constitute the doctrine were not met, and judgment for the defendants was affirmed.

Injuries Received During Disciplining

Consent to abuse cancels the liability of the act, and prevents later recovery for injuries the person who consented may have suffered. The courts have taken a hard-nosed approach to cases involving battery, and have barred recovery where no public policy is violated.

The attitude of the courts has not, in general, been one of paternalism. Where no public interest is contravened, they have left the individual to work out his own destiny, and are not concerned with protecting him from his own folly in permitting others to do him harm.

The consent must be to the act, not the resulting injury. The following example from the Restatement illustrates this point. A allows B to punch him as hard as he can in the chest. Unknown to A or B, A has a bad heart, and dies from the blow. Because the consent was effective, there was no liability created and thus no grounds for wrongful death.

Harsh conditioning and disciplining are inherent in the legitimate martial arts. An uncompromising military regime of belt ranks and absolute unquestioned authority reigns at the best martial arts dojo.

The style of conditioning is governed by the nature of the particular martial art. In judo, a repeated series of 100 falls to the mat strengthens the judoka's resistance to injury. In some forms of karate, conditioning is accomplished by *sanchin* breathing exercises. To toughen his midsection and ready it for an opponent's blows, a student practicing sanchin breathing locks his stomach muscles while his instructor pounds away with fists, feet and staffs.

Although prompted by a different motivation, discipline is delivered in a similar fashion. This includes body blows. In *Story v. Martin,* the defendant karate instructor maintained that striking the plaintiff after class was part of post-class disciplining. The defendant's witnesses testified that "a student of karate must expect rough treatment from his instructor, and that the instructor often physically disciplines the students during class." The defendant objected that the trial court did not allow enough evidence which might prove that karate instructors typically discipline students *after* class. Finding no evidence that the blow was related to karate instruction, the court upheld the verdict for the plaintiff. The important feature of *Story* is what the court did not do. Although it had the opportunity, the Louisiana Appeals Court did

According to the case *Story v. Martin,* student disciplining may be permitted in some states, as long as it takes place during normal class hours.

not condemn battery as it had occurred in dojo disciplining.

Legal issues arise concerning both martial arts conditioning and martial arts disciplining. The legal questions regarding conditioning are well illustrated with incidents involving sanchin breathing exercises. Consent to be hit doesn't include consent to be kicked. If a martial artist prepares himself for a fist to the abdomen, and receives instead an unexpected foot, a cause of legal action may exist. On the other hand, this "surprise kick" may be part of the package to which the plaintiff implicitly consented.

In regard to disciplining, *Story* gives attorneys for the defense some consolation. The instructor was held liable because the event took place during *post*-class disciplining. At least where children are involved, martial arts instructors will now be given clearer guidelines as to their privilege to discipline.

Coerced consent to conditioning or disciplining does not bar recovery by the "consenting" plaintiff. Thus, an instructor could not rely on a student's consent if the student was bullied into granting it.

Future of Martial Arts

Until recently, the few attempts that have been made to impose outside regulation on the martial arts have been successfully resisted. However, efforts *are* under way to change this. Self-regulation may remain viable, at least in the areas of training and competition, in those martial arts with strong central authorities. Judo stands the best chance of remaining self-regulated due to the effective leadership provided by the United States Judo Association (USJA), the United States Judo Federation (USJF), and the United States Judo, Inc. (USJI) These judo organizations report directly to the International Judo Federation, which is housed in Tokyo's Kokodan, "the home of judo."

Presently, there are few, if *any*, legal restrictions imposed on martial artists. The restrictions on boxers and wrestlers are much more stringent than those on martial artists. Any legislative attempt to regulate, license or register martial artists would face enforcement problems similar to those encountered by efforts at gun control. Black market and paperback instruction could prevent meaningful and even-handed enforcement of any limits on martial arts instruction.

Mandatory registration or licensure of martial artists is no solution. The capacity to employ deadly force shouldn't subject martial artists to any closer scrutiny than that given to those who carry a pocketknife. Because martial artists are trained to avoid street encounters, pocketknife carriers, as a class, may pose a greater threat than martial artists.

Proposal For Training Regulation

For several years, genuine martial artists and their con-man imitators have been free to open schools with no greater state involvement than that required to obtain a business license. In a poll of 26 dojo in various cities conducted in 1968, it was found that not even safety inspections are conducted at karate dojo. This seemingly careless government attitude has alarmed consumer groups and those fearful that martial arts studios may be converted into training grounds for muggers and unscrupulous thugs.

At least one state—Alabama—has responded. The state Attorney General's Office and the state Consumer Protection Agency were prepared to propose legislation to regulate martial arts in Alabama. These officers were concerned with the rip-off artists who offered substandard martial arts instruction to students trapped by confusing contracts. Karate leaders headed off these external regulations by forming the Alabama Martial Arts Association (AMAA), a non-profit organization to "regulate those persons who can teach the Martial Arts in Alabama, making them prove they are competent to carry their title." The regulation of martial artists by the AMAA parallels the regulation of lawyers by the ABA and physicians by the AMA.

Other private associations such as this should be organized. As of 1997, there exists no central state authority to set standards for martial arts instruction. Creating a guiding authority is the second-best way to upgrade and standardize martial arts instruction. The best method would be direct legislative interference—something few martial artists want. These new authorities or associations could establish requirements for certification. The potential teacher would have to demonstrate competence in the martial arts he wants to teach. This is better than automatic certification for martial artists who possess high-ranking belts, since it's no secret that sometimes belts are self-awarded, or awarded undeservedly. (This is especially true when a flim-flam man creates a "new style" of karate.) Certification would permit an instructor to teach students only with approval of the guiding association. Public service advertising could warn consumers of the dangers—both physical and economic—of enrolling in martial arts classes conducted by uncertified instructors. A certification fee could finance any administrative expenses.

CHAPTER
SEVEN

Death
by
Ninja

I n 1975, *ninja* were not very well-known and were not the focus of any American appellate cases. As of 1990, however, there were five reported cases which dealt with ninja. In four of these five cases,

Several appellate cases involved the dark trade of the ninja: murder.

murder was involved. Whether the criminal defendants were real or "wanna-be" ninja, each of the victims experienced the same fate—death.

Before considering how the American legal system treated ninja, a historical perspective is in order. As explained by Ashida Kim in his work *Secrets Of The Ninja:*

The word ninjitsu itself originated during a war between Prince Shotoku and Moriya over the land of Omi in sixth-century Japan. During this conflict a warrior named Otomo-no-Saajin contributed to the victory of Prince Shotoku by secretly gathering valuable intelligence about the enemy forces. For this service, he was awarded the title of Shinobi, which means "stealer-in." From this ideogram the character for ninjitsu is derived.

Ninja means "shadow warrior." The ninja of 17th-century Japan were family-oriented, and passed the tradition down to each generation as other families did with their respective trades. Like the son of the blacksmith, so too did the son (and daughter) of a ninja tend to become a ninja.

Training began at an early age, and it was rigorous. Ninja were expert martial artists whose killing skills were rivaled only by their ability to climb, conceal themselves and operate during the night. It is said "the night belongs to the ninja."

Ninja dress according to their environment, and use a variety of camouflage to suit their environment. The standard time of operation being night, the traditional outfit was completely ebon, with a small slit for the eyes. Most martial arts stores sell them. You've probably seen them at Halloween. These outfits, however, raise certain legal questions that will be discussed later.

Ninja basically have three traditional functions: to assassinate, to spy and to sabotage. The ninja dealt with in American courtrooms were assassins.

Ninja are hired guns. Individually and by family, ninja swore fealty to various warlords of yesteryear Japan. They jealously guarded their identity behind their black masks. It is said that ninja about to be captured would slice up their own face beyond recognition.

A hallmark of the ninja was perseverance. The story is told of a ninja family who was given the mission of assassinating a warlord rival to their own. The ninja pack attack scene in the television mini-series *Shogun* notwithstanding, ninja usually travel alone. So, first the father undertook the mission.

The warlord was well-prepared and well-protected. His castle was on high ground, surrounded by a series of moats emanating in concentric circles. Every tree and bush was cleared away so the warlord's retainers—samurai—could have maximum visibility, and the ninja could have minimum opportunity for stealth and hiding (which is known as the ninja art of *inpo*).

In approaching the warlord's well-fortified castle, the ninja employed the principle of *monomi-no-jitsu*, "observing the enemy from his perimeter." As samurai retainers approached, the father employed uzura gakaure no-jitsu, one of five hiding methods, which is suggestive of a small bird hiding in the small gaps in two other objects—in this instance, two rocks.

Unfortunately for him, the samurai were all too familiar with the ninja method of concealment. They scanned to see if any space was left empty between the rocks, and there was. Master though he was, assassin of three warlords, and murderer of countless lesser sentries and samurai, the ninja made a mistake. Moonlight could be seen shining through a small crack his elbow should have covered.

The samurai fell upon him with razor-sharp swords and hacked him to death. But he smiled as he died, knowing he had killed two men his wife would not have to deal with when she picked up the mantle he left for her.

The mother of the ninja clan went next and also failed, slain by a hail of arrows the samurai shot into the darkness at random each night.

The eldest brother also died, but he put himself within eyesight of the warlord whom he must kill before he was fallen upon by a sea of samurai hidden behind panels in the wall. This ninja killed nine samurai and wounded countless others before he fell.

Only the youngest son remained. His family's honor was at stake. Teenage Miyamoto started digging. For months he plunged his *ninja-to,* sword of darkness, into the hard earth, each time screaming silently, imagining the cold steel ripping into the warlord's chest.

Miyamoto was named after Japan's most famous swordsman, Miyamoto Musashi, who killed over 60 samurai before retiring to write the *Go Rin No Sho.*

Before their patriarch died, the ninja clan obtained a detailed map of the warlord's castle by bribing a disgraced *ronin* (samurai without a master). Miyamoto used this map with precision, measuring the tunnel by the length of his ninja-to. Therefore, he was not surprised when he found himself breaking through a wall of dirt directly under the warlord's private latrine.

Miyamoto returned there the next day, through the half-mile tunnel he created, with his sword of darkness, a long staff and rope, which he assembled into a deadly spear. He waited at the ready for hours, up to his waist in human feces and urine.

Even warlords have to relieve themselves, but it was a fatal mistake. As soon as Miyamoto saw light opening above him, replaced with pink flesh, he screamed as he drove the spear up though the warlord's rectum and stomach, between his lungs, and out his mouth. Death came quickly, too quickly, thought Miyamoto as he scrambled back through his tunnel. Swift, silent, deadly—these are the hallmarks of a ninja strike, Miyamoto reflected. His duty was discharged; the honor of his family was avenged.

Now there was a ninja for you.

This anecdote is important because criminals who commit crimes while wearing ninja outfits think they are ninja. They live in a shadowy world, a place the Japanese call the Void. As the following cases will show, in which 80 percent of them dealt with a ninja who committed murder, this is a very serious subject for the criminal justice system as well as the public at large.

Let us first look at the case of *State v. Evans*. John William Evans was a ninja, a real one. He was also a paranoid schizophrenic. That does not make his ninjitsu abilities less deadly, however. In fact, since ninja stalk the jagged edge of society, most true ninja would be labeled by society as mentally ill.

Evans, a ninja, committed three burglaries the night of December 1, 1980. He took "various and sundry items from the Elizabeth Lundblad, then Paul Cella homes. He took something else with him from the Janet Maitland residence; the ninja took her life." He had to kill that night.

Psychiatrist and expert witness John Borden testified that Evans "believed that he was 'a Ninja, a Japanese assassin,' that he 'felt he had to kill somebody,' and (t)hat he selected his neighbor woman and he knew he had a fairly good relationship with (her) on a realistic basis. He in a sense knew he would kill her sometime before this."

Borden made a confession to the police. His attention to detail validates his authenticity as a real McCoy shadow warrior:

(Evans) himself told the police that he had thought a lot about breaking into the victim's home, that as he crouched outside that night before going in, he pushed leaves over the shiny part of his boots, that he was wearing an army jacket together with the hood of a wet suit and a black scarf covering his face. Additionally, he stated that after he broke in and smoked a cigarette upstairs, he was careful to put the unsmoked portion in his pocket, that he wore gloves and never took them off until he left the house, that he pulled out the telephone jack and put it in another room to get it away from the victim.

Evans the ninja was lying in wait for Ms. Maitland. He did not go there to burglarize her home and then try to escape. He went there to kill. He killed her with his bare hands. He robbed her as an afterthought.

John Williams Evans was found guilty of felony-murder, and the conviction was upheld on appeal. Both the trial and appellate courts (with a dissent) held that Evans did not lack "substantial capacity to appreciate wrongfulness of his conduct."

Ironically, as the dissent of the appellate court pointed out, "During the defendant's hospitalization in January 1980, well before the occurrence of the crime of which he was convicted, the defendant had warned that he would 'kill someone,' and that he believed himself to be a 'ninja who had to kill.'"

Another Death By Ninja took place in Alaska. In the case of *Lewis v. State,* our ninja, Harry Lewis, was convicted of murder in the first degree and was sentenced to a maximum ninety-nine-year term of imprisonment. Lewis and his friend, Ricky Eason, met a dancer named Tamara Lynn Riley at PJ's, an Anchorage nightclub. Riley and Eason became romantically involved. The three of them plotted to kill Riley's husband so that Riley and Eason's affair could continue without interference from Riley's husband, and to receive a $35,000 life insurance policy.

In the case *Lewis v. State,* the defendant *ninja* apparently used *hadaka jime* (a stranglehold from behind that cuts off air between the lungs and the brain) to kill his victim.

The plot was hatched. Tamara called her husband, Leon Riley, from PJ's and asked that he come see her dance. She later called him and told him that Eason would give him a ride. Riley then advised her co-conspirators that all was set.

Lewis was the designated ninja.

In the words of the lower court, "Eason and Lewis drove in Lewis' van to the Rileys' apartment, and Lewis hid in the back of the van when Leon Riley got in. As Eason drove back toward PJ's, Lewis grabbed Riley by the throat from behind and strangled him. After disposing of the body, Eason and Lewis returned to PJ's and informed Riley that her husband was dead."

Lewis was dressed as a ninja when he strangled Riley to death. From the court's statement of facts, it appears that he killed him with the judo *shime waza* technique called *hadaka jime*, a stranglehold from behind that cuts off air between the lungs and the brain.

On appeal, Lewis' attorney argued that permitting expert testimony regarding the "legend of the Ninja assassins" prejudiced his client in the eyes of the jury.

The opinion recites:

At trial, Investigator Cox, who testified he was an expert in martial arts practice, explained his understanding of the Ninja as hired assassins, who dressed in black, hooded costumes. The state offered this evidence, coupled with evidence that Lewis wore a similar costume on the night of the homicide, to show Lewis' state of mind, i.e., that he perceived himself as a hired assassin.

The court rejected Lewis' argument and found "(t)he evidence was clearly relevant to explain Lewis' unusual attire and to establish his state of mind and intentions on the night of the murder."

Despite this being a first felony offense for Lewis and regardless that Lewis had a good military and employment record, with no discernible alcohol or drug problems, he was sentenced to ninety-nine years in prison, the maximum sentence for first-degree murder. On appeal, he argued that the sentence was excessive.

Ninja beware! This is how the appellate court responded:

We are satisfied that the trial court was not clearly mistaken in impos-

ing a maximum ninety-nine year sentence. In the present case, the trial court determined that Lewis had agreed to kill Riley, a stranger to him, for money, that he had carefully prepared for it, and that his actions were the worst kind of homicide: a willful, cold-blooded, contract killing. Under the circumstances, the trial court was justified in finding Lewis a worst offender based on the nature of his offense.

The third Death by Ninja case is *People v. Sledge.* John Sledge, the defendant, participated in a series of grocery robberies during Halloween on Brooklyn's Coney Island. He was dressed like a ninja.

At the fourth store, Sledge and others (50 to 60) met resistance as they tried to push their way into the grocery to steal eggs for throwing and beer for drinking. He shot and killed a store employee and was prosecuted for both second-degree intentional murder and second-degree felony-murder (since the killing took place during the commission of a felony (burglary of the store)).

The case revolved around neat legal questions concerning corroborating witness testimony and does not add anything substantive to legal questions involving ninja. However, it certainly is consistent with the fact that those dressed like ninja seem to be a killer breed. It adds to public concern and fear.

The final case does not involve murder. However, the Colorado Court of Appeals case of *People v. Jackson* instructs us about the consequences of dressing like a ninja.

The facts follow:

Two men were robbed and assaulted late at night by an individual dressed in dark clothes, including a mask and hood. Defendant was first noticed about three hours later, at approximately 1:45 a.m., by police officer Shelley Weber, who was driving a police car to a convenience store to assist other officers in an unrelated robbery incident. About a block before reaching the store, defendant crossed the street in front of her police car. He was dressed in a black Ninja costume, complete with mask, hood, shirt, long coat and pants. None of his features were visible except his eyes. When (Jackson) saw Weber's car, he ran. Weber pursued him, radioing for assistance. Defendant was chased by several police officers and eventually was arrested for trespassing after he was apprehended on a nearby motel roof. When he was searched following his arrest, police found items linking him to the crime for which he was convicted, including a credit card taken from the victim.

The ninja's lawyer argued that the court erred in not suppressing evidence since Officer Weber had no reason to pursue Jackson in the first place. The ninja's peculiar costume alone was not sufficient "to create the required reasonable suspicion of criminal activity."

The court did not buy it. "Here, (we have) a man dressed like a ninja warrior in the dead of night, who is heading away from a known crime scene and runs at the sight of a police car."

What can we learn from this handful of cases involving ninja? First of all, four of these cases involved murder and the fifth involved aggravated robbery, a crime of violence and third-degree assault. These various cold-blooded murders and assaults do nothing if not buttress the Hollywood caricature of the "ninja assassin."

Second, if you wear ninja garb and are charged with murder, the prosecution has precedence to bring in expert witnesses to recite the dark reputation and murderous legend of the Japanese ninja to show "state of mind at the time of the crime." *(Lewis).*

Third, stalking about while wearing a ninja outfit will give police some portion of the "probable cause" prerequisite for a constitutional search and seizure. *(Sledge).*

Fourth, the ninja cannot count on an automatic "not guilty by reason of insanity" verdict. *(Evans).*

Fifth and last, the American ninja assassin can expect no sympathy when sentencing takes place. *(Lewis: 99 years); (Woodman: death penalty. See Woodman v. Superior Court (People)).*

Although "the ninja does not leave tracks when he walks across the lake," black tabi footprints have marched across the pages of appellate opinions and probably will continue to do so. Thanks to the "invincible assassin" image they enjoy and the continuing desensitization to gore and death fostered by television and movies, ninja will continue to stalk in America.

One can only wonder how many ninja were never caught, and how many unsolved murders can be laid at the ebon feet of ninja never brought to justice.

CHAPTER EIGHT

Recommendations
and
Summary of
Advice

This book includes many suggestions for the courts and legislatures that someday will face questions similar to those contained herein. Some recommendations on how to deal with these complex issues are described in this chapter.

Martial Artist Liability Test (MALT)

This proposed test would be used by courts only where the martial artist is accused of assault and battery and cannot reasonably plead self-defense. The MALT test assumes that an assault and battery with the bare hands, feet (shoed or unshoed) or other animate part of an expert martial artist's body, when used skillfully to inflict injury, is a malicious attack. This test contains the following elements:

—Was the martial artist an expert?

—Was the injury caused by a technique which the martial artist knew or should have known as a result of training?

—Was the martial artist self-taught, or was he "trained" by other experts?

—Was the injury caused by a martial arts technique as opposed to "streetfighting?"

Application of this test creates a presumption that the assault was malicious, entitling the plaintiff to recover punitive damages. The martial artist can rebut the presumption with competent evidence that no martial arts technique was employed to commit the battery. MALT brings the law in focus with the reality of fighting arts and the ability of their practitioners to inflict severe injury by use of bare hands and feet.

Standard of the Reasonable, Prudent, Expert Martial Artist

Many times the reasonableness of the martial artist's conduct should be measured by his or her peers, not by the yardstick of the reasonable, prudent (lay)man. This seems particularly appropriate in the following areas:

1. *Reasonable Force.* A person is privileged to use reasonable force only in self-defense. Given the martial artist's ability to measure force with some precision, and to choose from a variety of possible defenses, the martial artist should be held to a higher standard of "reasonable force" than the non-martial artist. This should not be

confused with MALT. No presumptions of excessive force are raised. Unlike the (aggressor) martial artist who batters another, the martial artist employing self-defense has the legal process forced upon him or her.

2. *Anticipatory Attack.* A skilled martial artist knows when an assault is imminent. Under the doctrine of anticipatory attack, the martial artist is privileged to strike first. Whether this belief was reasonable should be determined by what a reasonable, prudent, expert martial artist would have done in the same or similar circumstances. The skill, training and reaction time of martial artists affect reasonableness to the anticipatory attack standard.

3. *Negligence.* Whether the martial artist's negligence caused the plaintiff's injuries raises a question of the martial artist's standard of care. The standard and its alleged infraction should be determined by looking to the martial artist's skill (when using the injurious technique) and belt rank. These considerations should go hand-in-hand with more traditional inquiries about negligence.

Duty To Warn

The Restatement imposes a duty to warn if one intends to use self-defense, assuming such warning will not escalate the severity of the assailant's attack. This duty to warn applies to martial artists as well as others. However, an expert martial artist should also warn a potential attacker about his special ability. This should help deter the attack, and it will not likely compromise the expert martial artist's self-defense. This expanded warning recognizes the camouflaged and greatly disproportionate ability of martial artists to injure an assailant.

Hands and Feet as Deadly or Dangerous Weapons

Hands, feet and other parts of the martial artist's body, when used skillfully, can be "deadly" or "dangerous" weapons within the eyes of the law. These animate instrumentalities should be considered weapons, with attendant consequences, when *used* like weapons.

Focusing on use rather than adoption of a *per se* rule—i.e., "the hands and feet of martial artists *are* deadly/dangerous weapons"— avoids two problems. First, a *per se* rule ignores the fact that martial artists can abstain from using martial arts techniques or can, at least, abstain from using *deadly* techniques. Second, a *per se* rule leads to a quagmire of undesirable results when carried to logical extremes. Namely: How does one *disarm* the unarmed martial artist? What effect would the *confiscation* (of deadly weapons) statutes have? Would martial artists be guilty of *concealing* a deadly weapon by keeping their hands in their pockets? The more reasonable approach seems to be that the *use* of the hands, feet, etc., determines whether the "deadly/dangerous weapon" characterization is justified.

Shoe considerations lose importance in cases hinging on whether the martial artist's feet were used as aggravated assault weapons. Since martial artists train in bare feet, often harden their bare feet, and many times can kick more effectively with bare feet, the judicial preoccupation with footwear should be secondary.

State registration of martial artists provides no solutions. The enforcement problem would be staggering; an equal protection question would be raised; and no important state interest would be significantly served.

Presumed Malice

Malice or specific intent will be presumed from the circumstances. Some would argue that when the defendant is a martial artist, his special skill calls for a presumption that the injury inflicted was the injury actually intended. If the martial artist is the undisputed aggressor, this presumption might be supported on public policy grounds. However, considerations shift when credible issues of self-defense exist. Unwittingly, the so-called "victim" may have exacerbated the injuries received from purely defensive techniques.

Martial artists should be allowed to rebut presumed malicious intent both with evidence of their personal reputations for peace and quietude; and with evidence that practitioners of their martial art are taught to use their skills only in self-defense.

Reasonableness Redefined to Reflect the Martial Artist's Special Training and Skill

Reasonableness underpins the privilege of self-defense. The issue is "reasonable according to whom?" Due to their unique abilities, martial artists should be judged by a unique standard. This will not always work to the martial artist's benefit, but it is more fair and realistic than treating the martial artist like a layperson. This special standard would apply in the following four situations:

1. *Apprehension and Fudoshin.* The basic self-defense requirement is that the defendant be "apprehensive" of bodily harm. Martial artists are trained to display fudoshin (calmness in an emergency), and this calmness could work to bar legitimate self-defense claims by martial artists. If peers are used to measure the martial artist's "apprehension," a valid self-defense claim can be asserted.

2. *General Reasonableness of Conduct.* While this standard as applied to "apprehension" clearly works to a martial artist's advantage, it just as clearly imposes a higher standard in terms of the overall reasonableness of the self-defense. Whether the martial artist can stop an assailant with less force than he actually used becomes important. Courts should be mindful of martial artists' special abilities, judging them by a "martial artist standard," and not sanction retribution guised as self-defense.

3. *Measurement of Force.* Defendants are entitled to use no more force in self-defense than is reasonably necessary. Unlike laypersons, martial artists can measure with some precision the force with which they apply their techniques. The only rational way to "test" this ability in the courtroom is by subjecting martial artists to the standard of their martial arts peers.

4. *Anticipatory Attack and Genshin.* Once the defendant reasonably knows an attack is imminent, he or she can "anticipatorily attack" in self-defense, inflicting the first blow. Enjoying a "radar attack system" cultivated by special training, the martial artist's genshin alerts him or her to the danger of attack. This is a prime example of the importance of the "reasonable according to whom?" question. While the martial artist's sudden anticipatory attack might appear unreasonable to a layperson, it probably would not to another martial artist. To avoid penalizing the martial artist for quick reaction time and a keen ability to perceive an imminent attack, martial artists should be judged by a standard of peers, not untrained counterparts.

Judicial Posture Toward Martial Artists

When confronted with a martial artist defendant, courts should determine his or her level of fighting competence before applying any presumptions or special standards. Experts should be distinguished from students or novices. Belt rank can be a useful, if sometimes mis-

Belt rank may be considered by the court when determining the defendant's level of fighting ability and therefore responsibility for the incident in question.

leading, rule of thumb. Black belts are clearly experts; brown belts may be. Professionally trained experts should be distinguished from self-taught or paperback-taught "experts." Novices, students and self-taught or paperback-taught martial artists usually possess insufficient proficiency to become the truly unique threat justifying unique treatment. Only the martial arts expert poses special problems for the criminal justice system.

Since criminal codes do not refer to any of the martial arts by name, no clear statutory guidelines exist to suggest the proper way for courts to deal with unarmed martial artists. Injustice will result if courts seize upon the defendant's status as a martial artist to support findings of "aggravated assault" or loss of the self-defense privilege due to "excessive force." Courts should examine facts. Relevant issues include: Is the defendant an expert martial artist? Did the defendant actually use a martial arts technique? If so, with what amount of force was the technique applied? Did the defendant deliberately strike or kick vulnerable areas on his adversary's body? To what extent did the acts of the injured party contribute to the injury incurred? Only when courts ask and find the answers to questions such as these will martial artists be treated justly.

CONCLUSION

This book assumes that current civil and criminal law lacks the legal theories and analyses to adequately cope with the issues posed by martial artists who can kill and maim without orthodox, inanimate weapons. Legal thought must expand, and lay to rest, questions raised by the advent of the martial arts. As Justice Cardozo explained, "The inn that shelters for the night is not the journey's end. The law, like the traveler, must be ready for the morrow. It must have a principle of growth." The law must grow to devise standards governing the conduct and legal defenses of the expert martial artist.

Many of the questions in this book are raised for the first time. If these questions, and the answers given here, stimulate others to tackle the difficult issues generated when martial artists and the law interact, then the effort has been worthwhile.

THE ELEVEN LEGAL
LESSONS TO
AMERICAN MARTIAL ARTISTS

The law lessons I hope this book imparts are these:

1. Consult a local lawyer as soon as there is the first hint of legal trouble. Consult about whether the lessons below hold true in **your** state. The legislature meets often and appellate courts hand down opinions every day. Do not rely on this book as dispositive.

2. Use just as much force as necessary, and not more, in self-defense. If someone pushes you and you retaliate by breaking bones and maiming, you may lose your "privilege of self-defense." However, if you are faced with deadly force—by gun, knife, club or martial arts weapon—you may respond with deadly force.

3. Have your lawyer check the law in your state with regard to martial arts weapons and legislative prohibitions and restrictions.

4. The fact that you are a trained fighter can be used for or against

201

you, as the cases cited in this book illustrate. However, more often than not, it will be a strike against you. Our reputations are exaggerated and Hollywoodized. These matters, that is to say, admissability into evidence of the martial arts defendant's status as such, may be addressed by pre-trial motion.

5. Whatever you do, don't drop into a martial arts stance when confronted by the law. You may be treated as a "deadly weapon." And shot.

6. When a student steps into the dojo or studio, he assumes that some violent activity will take place. He assumes certain risks. He may suffer some "expected injury," but he does not assume the risk he might be thrown between the mats onto a hard floor. Courts in negligence cases against martial arts instructors have taken into account "expert testimony" from other martial artists as well as applied traditional "reasonable, prudent man" negligence standards.

7. When it comes to sparring injuries during practice or at tournaments, the issue will come down to "consent" and whether contest rules were broken in the injury.

8. My prediction is that sooner or later some prosecuting attorney will indict one of us for "concealing a deadly weapon," i.e., our fighting ability when doing so "precipitated calamnity and mayhem." If you can do so without worsening the situation, advise the drunk in the bar you've just finished judo class and just want to go home after you swig down this last beer.

9. Walk away from conflict where possible. Some jurisdictions even impose a "duty to retreat." It is no show of cowardice to "flee with honor."

10. You may use the same force in defending another as you could use had you yourself been attacked.

11. The eleventh lesson is to walk humbly. This is the smart martial artist's best way to avoid conflict.

TABLE OF CASES

Chapter 1: The Martial Arts
none

Chapter 2: Assault and Battery

Commonwealth v. Buzard 76 A.2d 394 (Pa. 1950)
Quarles v. State 204 S.E.2d 467 (Ga.App 1974)
State v. Johnson 300 S.W. 207 (Mo. 1927)
Lyon v. Commonwealth 239 S.W. 207 (Mo. 1927)
Vogg v. Commonwealth 239 S.W.2d 86 (Ky. 1948)
State v. Born 159 N.W.2d 283 (Minn. 1968)
State v. Golladay 470 P.2d 191 (Wash. 1970)
Pulliam v. State 298 So.2d 711 (Miss. 1974)
State v. Broten 176 N.W.2d 827 (Iowa 1970)
Acres v. United States 164 U.S. 388 (1896)
Dickson v. State 323 S.W.2d 432 (Ark. 1959)
Bass v. State 172 So.2d 614 (Fla. 1965)
Johnson v. State 249 So.2d 452 (Fla. 1971)
United States v. Barber 297 F.Supp 917 (D.C. Del. 1969)
State v. Bradley 116 N.W.2d 439 (Iowa 1962), cert.
denied 374 U.S. 490 (1963)
Medlin v. United States 207 F.2d 33 (D.C. Cir. 1953), cert.
denied 347 U.S. 905 (1954)
Ransom v. State 460 P.2d 170 (Alaska 1969)
People v. Zankich 11 Cal.Reptr. 115 (Cal. 1961)
People v. Fuentes 169 P.2d 391 (1946)

Chapter 3: Martial Artists and the Presumption of Deadly Ability

Presumption of Martial Artists Deadly Ability to Inflict Injury
People v. Dabney 422 N.Y.S. 2d 116 (1973)
422 N.Y.S. 2d 116 (1981)
N.Y., 420 N.E.2d 81 (1981)
People v. Corbett Colo., 611 p.2d 965 (1980)
State v. McNish 727 S.W.2d 490 (Tenn. 1987)
State v. O'Connell 275 N.W.2d 197 (Iowa 1979)
People v. Ward 233 Cal. Rptr. 477 (Cal. App. 5 Dist. 1986)
Williams v. State Nev., 603 P.2d 694 (1979)
State v. Morse Me., 394 A.2d 285 (1978)
State v. Jarrell 608 P.2d 218 (1980)

Martial Artists In Chains
Commonwealth v. Montgomery 499 N.E.2d 853 (Mass. App. Ct. 1986)

Chapter 4: Martial Arts and the Law of Self-Defense

The Requirement of Apprehension

The Restatement of Torts, 2d

The Duty to Warn

The Duty to Retreat

The Question of "Excessive Force"

6 AM JUR 162

Lyon v. Commonwealth	239 S.W.1046 (Ky. 1922)
Gober v. State	219 P.173 (Ok. Cr. 1923)
Etter v. State	205 S.W.2d 1 (Tenn. 1947)
State v. McLeod	870 N.E.2d (Ohio App. 1948)
Jones v. Commonwealth	256 S.W.2d 520 (Ky. 1953)
People v. Atkins	276 N.E. 21 36 (Ill. App. 1971)
Davis v. State	51 N.E. 928 (IN 1898)
State v. Hopkins	213 S.W. 126 (Mo. 1914)

Anticipatory Attack

State v. Evans	208 S.E.2d 283 (N.C. App. 1923)
State v. Daugherty	196 S.W.2d 627 (Mo. 1946)

Deadly Force Against A Trained Fighter

Wilson v. State	548 S.W.2d 323 (Tenn. 1977)
State v. Horton	263 S.E.2d 745 (N.C. 745)
State v. Glenn	485 So.2d 629 (La. App. 4 Cir 1986)
State v. Nielsen	280 N.W.2d 904 (Neb. 1979)
Echizenya v. Armenio	354 So. 2d 682 (La. App. 1978)

Prejudice Against the Martial Artist

Commonwealth v. Oram	457 N.E.2d 284 (Mass. App. 1983)

Chapter 5: Martial Arts Weapons and the Law: What's Legal In Your State?

State v. Mulifu	64 HAW. 485, 643 P.2d 546, 549 (1982)
Commonwealth v. Adams	245 PA. Super. 431, 369 A.2d, 479, 482 (1976)

Judicial Interpretation of State Statutes Pertaining to Martial Arts Weapons

In Re. S.P.	465 A.2d. 823 (D.C.App. 1983)
Tatom v. State	Tx.Ct.Crim.Ap., 555 S.W.2d. 459
Toledo v. Texas	651 S.W.2d. 382 (Tex.App. 2d.Dist. 1983)
People v. Tate	Ill. App., 386 N.E.2d. 584 (1st Dist. 1979).
City of Pekin v. Shindledecker	*Ill.App.,* 426 N.E.2d. 13 (3rd Dis. 1981)
People v. Malik	245 N.W.2d. 434 (1976)
State v. Mitchell	371 N.W.2d. 432 (Iowa App. 1985)
R.V. v. State	497 So.2d. 913 (Fla.App. 3 Dist. 1986)
State v. Tucker	Or.App., 558 P.2d. 1244 (1977)

People v. White	425 N.W.2d. 193 (Mich.App. 1988)
State v. Lupien	466 A.2d. 1172 (Vt. 1983)
State v. Mullen	N.C.App., 280 S.E.2d. 11 (1981)
In re Reed	Wash.App., 583 P.2d. 1228 (1978)
People v. Wethington	460 N.E.2d. 856 (Ill.App.3 Dist. 1984)
State v. Maloney	470 N.E.2d 211 (Ohio App. 1984)

Commonwealth v. Adams Pa.Super. 369 A.2d. 479 (1976)

Keastead v. Commonwealth of Pa. Bd. of Probation & Parole
514 A.2d. 265 (Pa.Cmwlth. 1986)

State of Hawaii v. Muliufi	643 P.2d. 546 (1982)
Toledo v. State	Tex.App., 631 S.W.2d. 825 (1982)
State v. Beeman, Iowa	315 N.W.2d. 770 (1982)
People v. Olsen	514 N.E.2d. 233 (Ill.App. 2 Dist. 1987)
Cole v. State of Oklahoma	Okla.Cr., 569 P.2d. 470 (1977)

Commonwealth v. Chandler Ky. 722 S.W.2d. 899 (1987)

State v. Sanders	748 S.W.2d. 835 (Mo.App. 1988)
City of Columbus v. Dawson	501 S.E.2d. 77 (Ohio App. 1986)
People v. Mott	522 N.Y. S.2d. 429 (Co.Ct. 1987)
Taylor v. U.S.	848 F.2d. 715 (6th Cir. 1988)
Vaughn v. State	470 N.E.2d. 374 (Ind.App. 4 Dist. 1984)
Albert v. State of Texas	659 S.W.2d. 41 (Tex.App. 14 Dist. 1983)
Hayes v. State of Texas	672 S.W.2d. 246 (Tex.App. 9 dist. 1984)
McQueen v. State	362 S.E.2d. 436 (Ga.App. 1987)
Masters v. State	653 S.W.2d. 944 (Tex.App. 3 Dist. 1983)
Commonwealth v. Brown	Pa., 414 A.2d. 70 (1980)

Chapter 6: Martial Arts Sports Injuries: Assumption of Risk and the Effect of Consent

4 AM. Jur. 2d.	Amusements & Exhibitions sec 866 (1962)
Prosser on Torts	(4th Ed., 1971) at sec. 18

The Restatement of Torts sec. 50, comment b.

Restatement, Tent. Draft sec. 892A, Note to Institute

Nicholls v. Colwell	113 Ill.App. 219 (1904)
Gibeline v. Smith	1066 Mo.App. 545, 80 S. W. 961 (1904)
McNeil v. Mullin	70 Kan 634, 79 P. 168 (1905)
Fitzgerald v. Cavin	110 Mass. 153 (1872)

Injuries Inflicted By A Sparring Partner or Contest Opponent

Kuehner v. Green	436 So.2d. 78 (Fla. 1983)
Scogin v. Century Fitness, Inc.	6A C.J.S. sec. 17

Injuries Received During "Mutual Combat"

Matthews v. Ollerton	noted by Prosser at sec. 18
McAdams v. Windham	208 Ala. 492, 94 So. 742 (1922)
Lewis v. Fountain	168 N.C. 277, 84 S.E. 278 (1915)
Shay v. Thompson	59 Wis. 540, 18 N.W. 473 (1884)
Teolis v. Moscatelli	44 R.I. 494, 119 a. 161 (1925)
Grotton v. Glidden	84 Me. 589, 24 A. 1008 (1892)

Injures Caused By the Negligence of the Instructor

Klocek v. YMCA of Metro Milwaukee	48 Wis.2d 43, 179 N.W.2d 835 (1970)
Wells v. Colorado College	478 F.2d 158 (1973)
Fantini v. Alexander	N.J., 410 A.2d 1190 (1980)
Brown v. Bridges	Fla.App., 327 So.2d 874 (1976)
Jackson v. Washington State Criminal Justice Training Commission	720 P.2d 457 (Wash.App. 1986)

Injures Received During Disciplining

Story v. Martin	La.App. 217 So.2d 758 (1969)

Chapter 7: Death By Ninja

State v. Evans	523 A.2d 1306 (Conn. 1987)
Lewis v. State	731 P.2d 68 (Alaska App. 1987)
People v. Sledge	519 N.Y.S. 2d 185 (Sup. 1987)
People v. Jackson	742 p.2d 929 (Colo. App. 1987)
Woodman v. Superior Court (People)	241 Cal.Rptr. (818) 2 Dist. (1987)